Praise for

When the Stork Passes By: A Field Guide to Practical Compassion

"Dr. Julie Shannon approaches a delicate subject as one who knows from personal experience, and yet this is more than just one person's story. She gives voice to so many who have not known exactly how to address their own questions and emotions, and she does so poignantly. Her insights are penetrating, her encouragements are real, her suggestions are spot on. Her audience is not only the women who have travelled the path of infertility, but loved ones sharing the experience, professionals working alongside, church and community members wanting to know how to help. You will feel blessed as you read this necessary book."

—Dr. Les Carter, author and psychotherapist

"It's almost impossible to truly enter deeply into someone else's pain, but needed to actually understand and minister to them— or to experience that someone else actually "gets" what they are feeling, alleviating that horrible sensation of being completely alone. Dr. Shannon takes us into the depths of her excruciating journey through years of roller-coaster infertility and childlessness, but she doesn't leave us curled up in a fetal position in the corner. God is redeeming her agonizing disappointment by opening doors for her to minister to others through her writing, counseling, and speaking. *When the Stork Passes By* offers hope for childless couples, showing them how to find fruitful purpose-filled lives despite their unfulfilled longings. And it provides insight and guidance for family, friends, community, the church, and health professionals to help them avoid unintentionally twisting the knife in childless couples' wounds. But this book is more than one woman's voice and experience—it's research based, revealing multiple voices of other childless women. Will any of them ever get over their sadness of never being a mom? No, but they all explain who and what God used to propel them through their disappointment to a life of purpose and fulfillment. For anyone touched by infertility and childlessness, this book is a priceless resource that can transform the journey of countless couples who have watched the stork pass them by but choose a different path to a fruitful life."

—Dr. Sue Edwards
Professor of Educational Ministries and Leadership
Dallas Theological Seminary
Author of The *Discover Together Bible Study* series and
co-author of six leadership books for women

"If only someone had given us a few helpful clues on how to navigate infertility the way our moms did about how to tell a salad fork from the dessert fork. Instead, among Christians, infertility is a self-imposed 'taboo topic.'

In *When the Stork Passes By*, Dr. Julie Shannon delivers just the right stuff. Julie has written out of personal travail and significant professional training. The way she narrates her own story draws one in no matter how infertility has touched their life. If you live with the burden of infertility, expect Julie to personalize your pain while helping you process the anger and resentment you carry for those added wounds received from family, friends, and foes. Maybe you are a lay person caregiver, or you are a pastoral staffer, or even a high skills clinician. In any case you will find yourself putting *When the Stork Passes By* in lots of hands. Because this book is that good!"

—Dr. Willie O. Peterson
Assistant to the Superintendent,
Midsouth Conference, Evangelical Covenant Church
Adjunct Professor, Dallas Theological Seminary
Doctor of Ministry Studies

"We need one another. Yet, sometimes we don't know what to say or do. Or worse, we might compound a person's despair with careless comments intended to make light of a painful reality. How do you respond to someone experiencing childlessness? Julie Shannon has taken her personal anguish, harnessed it, and mobilized herself for ministry to this precious population. She candidly writes of the impact of childlessness and the insensitivity of others toward it. Her tips may help you avoid an embarrassing or hurtful word or action in the future."

—Michelle Attar
Pastor of Adult Ministries
Bent Tree Bible Fellowship, Carrollton, Texas

"My wife and I have been good friends with Julie for a number of years. Her writing exudes biblical fidelity, careful thought and a wealth of practical experience with the problems she discusses. She refers to them as 'silent topics in a noisy world.' Her audience is infertile Christian couples, who face ignorance and a lack of empathy in their struggles with grief and loneliness. As the father of children who struggled with infertility, I understand the urgent need for Julie's book. With practical acumen she guides her readers through medical, spiritual, and relational hurdles toward a meaningful life 'in comforting others with encouragement from the God of compassion.'"

—Dr. Lanier Burns
Research Professor, Theological Studies
Dallas Theological Seminary

When the Stork Passes By:

A Field Guide to Practical Compassion

Dr. Julie Shannon

Print: 978-1-7341776-3-3
Ebook: 978-1-7341776-4-0
Audio: 978-1-7341776-5-7

Library of Congress Control Number: 2020910897

Scripture quotations are taken from the New American Standard Bible® (NASB), Copyright © 1960, 1962, 1963, 1968, 1971, 1972, 1973, 1975, 1977, 1995 by The Lockman Foundation, Used by permission. www.Lockman.org.

Front cover image by Dr. Julie Shannon
Front and back cover design by Brad Wofford, BW Design
Interior drawings by Ben Humeniuk
Edited by Kelley Mathews
Formatting by Polgarus Studio

Printed by Shannon Communication, LLC, in the United States of America.

First printing and ebook edition 2020.

www.drjulieshannon.com

Dedicated to the women who shared their stories with me.

Thank you for the courage to open up your heart and memories about deep pain and wounds in the realm of infertility and childlessness—many of you for the very first time.

Your voice will be used to transform lives and situations. Your sharing will help others know how to help their friends and loved ones. May God fill you to overflowing with His joy in all of the fruit you are bearing in your life.

This is a work of nonfiction and the culmination of research, interviews, and conversations experienced by the author. The first names related to real life situations are pseudonyms created by the interviewees to protect their privacy and in some cases, to honor their lost or desired children.

The author offers advice based on her experience and/or wisdom gleaned from others. She is neither a medical doctor nor a financial planner, and this book should not be used as a substitute for professional consultation and advice from the appropriate medical or business expert.

Contents

Foreword

As I write this, the daily post has been delivering stacks of Christmas photos. I would say Christmas *cards*, except that we don't actually receive too many cards any more. Instead, the typical stack of mail contains no-fold cardstock pages full of others' family *photos*. I enjoy seeing how my friends with, say, four kids have gone on to become in-laws (make that eight) and then grandparents—some of whom are up to sixteen now. I rejoice for them. I honestly do. Yet I also often feel that wistful sense of "what might have been" for us. The sensation soon passes. But I'm sure it will always catch me by surprise in unexpected moments.

The "what might have been" stems from the reality that my husband (of forty years now) and I endured a decade of infertility that included years of no success, seven early pregnancy losses, three failed adoptions, a successful adoption, and the grand finale of an ectopic pregnancy. At the time when all that was happening, few helps existed to guide us through the first major ethical, marital, financial and spiritual crisis in our marriage. In the years that have followed, I've been happy to see the cobbled-together resources morph into an abundance of options. But some of the last helps to become available have been those designed for people wanting to support those who endure infertility and involuntary childlessness.

One of the most meaningful things anyone did for me during our decade wandering in the desert was to read a book about infertility (wading through chapters on FSH and LH and HCg and Clomid and Pergonal and IVF) so she could better understand my pain. That person was my mother—whose own fertility journey lay at the opposite end of the spectrum. She birthed five children, of whom I was the fourth. And for her, the last two kids were surprises that meant she never did get to finish college and become a teacher. She was too busy raising a musician, an artist, an educator, a writer, and a modiste. Nevertheless, instead of saying bitterly to me, "Enjoy your higher-ed opportunities," she wept with me, empathized about burying dreams, and did all she could to help shoulder my losses.

The book you hold in your hands (or on your device) is the resource I wish I could have given her then. Its author, my dear friend Dr. Julie Shannon, has given of herself generously, drawing on her own heartache to make life easier for those coming behind her on the path. Dr. Julie speaks as someone who has truly "been there." But rather than relying only on her own narrative, she has earned master's and doctoral degrees—both from a theological seminary—so she can credibly exegete and apply Scripture, as well. Today as she ministers both to those who hurt and those who help the hurting, she adds to her own incredible story an intimate knowledge of the Bible, thousands of hours spent listening to others who are childless, and medical and psychological research. Her voice is one of credibility and compassion.

A wise man once wrote, "Like apples of gold in settings of silver, so is a word skillfully spoken" (Prov. 25:11). Here in the pages of *When the Stork Passes By* you'll find an entire gallery of skillfully spoken words, crafted especially for a unique setting. May you, as you internalize and apply them, be used of God to help those who hurt make out of their ashes something of beauty.

—Dr. Sandra Glahn
Co-author of *When Empty Arms Become a Heavy Burden*
and *The Infertility Companion*
December 2019

Introduction
A Journey Transformed

God blessed them; and God said to them, "Be fruitful and multiply, and fill the earth, and subdue it; and rule over the fish of the sea and over the birds of the sky and over every living thing that moves on the earth."
(Genesis 1:28, NASB)

The journey of infertility isolates many individuals and couples.

Infertility presents physical, emotional, relational, financial, and spiritual challenges. Those within the community, church, and other faith organizations must gain an understanding of the infertility impact in order to minister to this particular hurt and need, act as God's instruments of healing, and love one another.

The Christian church emphasizes the growth of family, embodied in the fertility of couples, as an answer to "be fruitful and multiply" (Genesis 1:28). Sermons often lift up the biblical stories of Hannah, Sarah, and Elizabeth as evidence of God's blessing through the matriarchs' eventual fruitfulness in bearing children. Proceed with care when digging into biblical stories, meaning, and "advice."

Loving one another requires empathy with and support for fellow believers in their pain of infertility and childlessness through guidance and hope, encouraging vitality in a well-lived life, spiritual transformation, and discipleship.

Infertility generally means difficulty getting pregnant or staying pregnant after one year of unprotected sexual intercourse. The Office on Women's Health within the US Department of Health & Human Services indicates that ten percent of American women aged 15–44 suffer from infertility. Twenty percent have their first child after age thirty-five. When the woman is over thirty-five, one-third of couples experience challenges with fertility. [1]

Postponing childbirth directly affects the increase in fertility issues. According to Pew Research, a growing number of Millennials will face infertility due to their delay in marriage.[2] The reality of today's current trends will influence the need for future infertility and childlessness outreach in the church and community.

When a married couple decides to start their family and pregnancy does not occur, a subtle layer of stress begins. As time passes with no pregnancy or with pregnancy followed by miscarriage, emotions often rise and despair follows. The more couples try, and—in their minds—fail, the more they require support from members of their community.

Unfortunately, the pain and humiliation of infertility may create a cocoon of privacy and disconnection that isolates couples from friends, family, and their faith community. Judith Stigger opens a window into the unique mourning of infertility:

> Infertile couples often grieve alone. When a person loses a living relative, other family and friends know: they gather to console and support. Talking of the loss and receiving expressions of caring from others helps the person absorb and accept the event. The opportunity to "talk it out" is an aid to healing. In contrast, no one but the spouse and physician may be aware of the loss of an "assumption child."[3]

Miscarriage and stillbirth occurrences are not singular events that a person briefly passes through. In a post on the *Still Standing Magazine* site, a woman named Catherine shares her grief reality:

> It is lonely. I can't deny it. Four years on, I sometimes suspect that hardly anybody grieves for Georgina as I still do. The child who I once held safe inside my body, enclosed and protected. I think that we all grieve the loss of potential here, a child that might have been. And it's hard to explain to others what we mourn for. A baby, a child, a teenager, a young woman or man, an adult, their children, their old age, their grandchildren. Worlds upon worlds of loss. Because if your baby does not survive birth, or infancy, or is never to be at all, that is what vanishes. A world in its entirety.[4]

To be effective, a minister must understand the lifelong ramifications of such losses. The Body of Christ is called to love God, love one another, and make disciples.

I experienced seven years of infertility challenges that included three miscarriages. The motherhood dream I nurtured for life never came to fruition; emotional and spiritual paralysis followed.

Thankfully, I journeyed with a trusted group of friends experiencing similar circumstances, and we supported one another. But even in this circle of incredible encouragement, I experienced a deep hollowness that slowed the process of discerning God's plan after the death of my dream.

One of the pastors from our church also assisted me in spiritual recovery. Slowly, I began to make peace with my new reality, and a path opened up for me to help women and communities through the fallout of infertility.

As my window of opportunity for childbearing narrowed, I surrendered to my reality. I began searching desperately for some book or resource to tell me life would be okay, that the loss of my dream would not mean a fruitless life with nothing but ashes and devastation on the path ahead.

Every written word I devoured on the page or screen led to a new level of defeat. I encountered many who walked the same road to a point, but every story seemed to end with a child, either biologically or by adoption.

As I traveled through this time and eventually on to graduate school, I begrudgingly allowed my heart to soften toward the possibility that I needed to speak truth in love and humor to others on how to revive their life after the loss of this dream and during the chaotic walk of infertility.

I finally said yes to God and began to explore opportunities to help others in the midst of infertility. While developing workshops, I conducted focus groups, gathered feedback, and uncovered a key source of hurt for those in the midst of infertility and those who were involuntarily childless.

The very communities needed to support loved ones in this struggle (family, friends, and others) often unintentionally fail to enfold these couples in loving and practical compassion.

The very communities needed to support loved ones often unintentionally fail to enfold these couples in loving and practical compassion.

Sojourners on earth need to come alongside family members in the church to console siblings and offer the whisper of encouragement that life holds meaning and a great plan for all.

This book includes information from one-on-one research interviews with married women in the church who wanted children, could not have them, and did not raise children in their home.

These discussions shed light on who or what God used to propel such women through the loss of their dreams toward grabbing hold of his plan for their fruitful life. We focused on the following problem: how married women who are involuntarily childless due to infertility have found true value and meaning in life.

The interviews explored how women without children
- found value in understanding biblical truth about their identity, purpose, and gifts;
- found meaning in community;
- found meaning in helping others in need.

All of this information enhances ministry to women and couples who experience infertility and childlessness.

We will see how women were equipped to walk well through their infertility journey and beyond and draw suggestions and positive actions from their experiences.

Churches can be true family for those members who cannot produce their own by enfolding them in community, and by equipping those in the community with a practical course of action. They can learn what to say and do, and develop a sense of understanding and compassion.

Primarily, I sought to discover who or what God used to propel childless women through their pain to a life of purpose and fulfillment.

Information garnered from participant interviews provided helpful direction to loved ones, community, and the church interacting with people currently in the midst of infertility and especially to those who have no children. Interviewees shared helpful actions that meet the needs of the infertile and childless during times of confusion and disappointment.

Interview questions revolved around the individual dream of having a child and how they faced the following:

Medical experience
Physical challenges
Spiritual dilemma
Relational predicaments

We looked at how the women distilled their emotions and effectively utilized connections or support systems. We identified people and events that God used to encourage the participants, and how they discovered their purpose, their new life roles, and the impact of social events.

We discussed past and present reactions about the yearly impact of Mother's Day and different seasons of reliving the loss throughout life (high school graduations, marriages, grandchildren, etc).

The interview answers revealed a bridge between the heartbreak of infertility and childlessness and healing with the help of local church, ministry, and community. Each woman chose her pseudonym for the interview and that name is used in this book as well. Touchingly, most of the first names they declared were ones they intended to give their children.

For clarity, I've included a few definitions of frequently used terms we will encounter during our time together:

Infertility

Essentially, infertility is defined as the inability to conceive and carry to term after one year of unprotected sex. Numerous variables such as medical conditions and age add layers to the general definition. According to the American Society for Reproductive Medicine (ASRM), women thirty-five years and older are considered infertile after six months of unprotected sex.[5]

The Mayo Clinic and other sources show an infertility percentage rate of ten to fifteen percent for couples of childbearing age in the United States.[6] Through this reading I will refer to an "active infertility season," and by this I mean the timeframe in which a woman actively pursues pregnancy and childbirth. This also includes the season of grieving when raw emotions flare up during the process of moving forward.

Childless

The term childless or childlessness within our discussions refers to those who want children, do not have children, and are not raising children in their home—involuntary childlessness.

Childfree is a term used by those who choose not to have children—voluntary childlessness. Transitioning from a barren or "less" mentality is necessary in order to live a full life, but the "less" often remains an inner lens through which many infertiles view life. Hope moves the barren into a stage of fruitfulness through other means.

For example, I am missing the presence of the children I miscarried, the children who will never be. I choose to trust God and seek his will and a "full" or fruitful life, but I will never escape, nor do I want to, the child-hollow deep inside.[7]

Sandra Glahn and William Cutrer present and label a childfree transition:

> It has been said that there are two kinds of couples without children: those who are childfree by chance and those who are childfree by choice. But there's another group—those who start out in the first group but slowly embrace the second. They begin by calling themselves childless, but eventually they choose to use the label "childfree."[8]

I tell others I will never "get over" not having a child. I will never be okay with not being a mom. No longer do I wallow in the bitterness, but I realize that deep down there is a foundational piece of myself that grew out of my season of infertility and miscarriages.

My inability to forget or to let go of this small corner of who I am allows me to call upon the pain and healing in order to share, counsel, and continue to grow in life. Those of us on the infertility and childless path must choose to *live* and incorporate the experience into our lives.

Church Family

Members of local churches and other believers worldwide make up the universal family of God. Every believer in Jesus Christ makes up the church, the Body of Christ, and we are co-heirs in God's kingdom (Romans 8:16–17; 1 Corinthians 12:12–14; Ephesians 3:15).

Often the local church emphasizes individual family units to the exclusion of the overarching family of God.

Author Joseph Hellerman illuminates the biblical family structure:

> For Jesus, Paul, and early church leaders throughout the Roman Empire, the preeminent social model that defined the Christian church was the strong-group Mediterranean family. God was the Father of the community. Christians were brothers and sisters. The group came first over the aspirations and desires of the individual. Family values—ranging from intense emotional attachment to the sharing of material goods and to uncompromising family loyalty—determined the relational ethos of Christian behavior.[9]

Community

The people in the settings of our lives make up our community. We experience the facets of community where we work, live, and worship—the intertwining of our lives and activity become community.

On a larger scale, community is the city, state, country in which we live. It becomes the nurturing, affirming intentional people in our lives who accompany us on our earthly journey.

Fruitful

A fruit-laden tree indicates healthy production. The fruitful reference in Genesis 1 refers to bearing children, multiplying God's people through birth. In the Sermon on the Mount (Matthew 7), Jesus illustrates the manner in which true teachers (followers) could be identified—by their fruit: "You will know them by their fruit" (7:20). New Testament living offers a witness of the love of God through Christ—fruit production: "So that you will walk in a manner worthy of the Lord, to please Him in all respects, bearing fruit in every good work and increasing in the knowledge of God" (Colossians 1:10).

Lydia Brownback describes the biblical idea of bearing fruit. She writes, "In the old covenant, God built a people for himself by means of human procreation (Gen. 15:1–6). In the new covenant, the emphasis is on building God's spiritual family

11

through union with Christ, yet the biological family retains its
high value (see e.g., John 19:26–27; Eph. 5:22–6:4; Titus 2:3–
5; 1 Peter 3:1–7)."[10]

How many children do you have?

When are you going to give me grandchildren?

Why don't you have any children?

These questions pierce the hearts of married couples trying to
conceive and have a child. The speaker means no harm and does
not realize the pain these questions deliver.

Infertility and miscarriage are silent topics in a noisy world.
Church culture tends to revolve around families, and resources
for couples in the lonely pain of infertility are not widely
available, especially for those who are involuntarily childless.

Those who do not have children may exist on the fringes of
church life, feeling unworthy and neglected. New compassion
and understanding equips the church to reach out to her
members, helping them live vibrantly and discover ways in which
God wants to use them. Including them in the church family
helps move them out from under their burden of grief.

Due to my experience with the infertility journey I often face
questions about what to do for someone suffering through this
season. As we interact candidly throughout this book you will

become better equipped to provide practical assistance and compassion to your loved ones in infertility.

Consider this book the emotional advocate for your daughter or son, sister, brother, or friend on the infertility journey. Please take everything with a helping of love and sincere gratitude that you care and want to give them your support.

Much of the emotional pain for infertile couples, especially women, comes from the people closest to them. I say women especially because women in infertility are most affected by the realm of social conventions that provokes pangs of grief—shopping malls, baby showers, social media pregnancy and birth announcements.

Men are affected through these same avenues of hurt. They will benefit from the experiences and thoughts here, but many examples and stories will naturally flow from my own experience as well as from conversations and focus groups with women.

Women need new practices, procedures, and loving action from their community members. Implementing them results in practical compassion for women in the midst of infertility and transformation of their isolation and pain.

The women I interviewed for this book's research all have a Christian faith/church background, current involvement in Christian leadership, ministry, church, or seminary. They are involved in Bible study leadership, music programs, juvenile ministry work, communication ministry, teaching, church leadership, church pastor, and mentoring.

Each woman struggled through an active infertility season (actively trying to get pregnant, medical procedures, tests, etc.). Some struggled as recently as five years ago, some as long as twenty-plus years ago. Their ages ranged from forty-five to seventy-eight years old. Their history involved not only pregnancy losses, but also miscarriage and infant loss, and also an inability to get pregnant, many times with no medical diagnosis or answer as to why.

Note: Infertility pain never completely disappears. New life seasons bring new opportunities. For example, the older interviewees still struggle with regular reminders—back-to-school pictures, school graduations, weddings, baby showers, and eventually the reality of nonexistent grandchildren.

Some of these women have not and do not currently attend church on Mother's Day (every one of the interviewees experienced some level of emotional discomfort on Mother's Day).

Some of them struggle with baby showers—many will not attend, many will not attend but will send a gift with someone else. Those who *do* attend them are extremely selective.

None of the interviewees indicated participation with a formal infertility support group during or after their active infertility season.

Several had a friend or family member who reached out during their infertility crisis, but less than half experienced church outreach. When asked if they, as involuntarily childless couples in the church, were currently supported and included by church community, activities, and ministries, *half answered no.*

Throughout the book you will see the following interactive elements:

 — Tools/Suggestions: What to do?

 — Helpful direction/guidance: Where to go?

 — Take a breather, reflection: Why?

Individual Journeys

Everyone's story is a different journey with a different ending. While every adventure maps in a unique way, most include an element of struggle in the following areas: physical, emotional, spiritual, relational.

This book will help you avoid unintentionally hurting those whom the stork passes by.

This book will equip you to help others in their (ongoing, ever-changing) pain and need.

Thanks for joining me.

Let's go...

Chapter 1
A Fellow Traveler's Tale

"This is no longer a viable fetus. I see no heartbeat."

Turbulence overwhelms me as her pronouncement pummels the quiet. Impersonal cold about the peanut whose heart I saw racing weeks ago.

Lying on the table, I realize the "fabric of our lives" cotton sheet draped over me offers no protection against this assault.

Words that catapult me into chaos require preparation, yet she neglected even a cushion to soften the blow. At thirty thousand feet, passengers at least hear a warning to buckle up before the plane drops out from under them.

My heart takes a breath.

Pauses.

One thousand-one. One thousand-two. One thousand-three.

I fold inward like a compressed accordion whose bellows have exhaled for the last time.

Defeat taps my heart and fissures wend through every molecule—creating crackle most decorators would envy.

Why don't I hear *code blue*? Bile rises in the back of my throat as I realize the devastation resides in my spirit.

My heart beats.

So began the end of my willingness to continue the childbearing quest. This third and final loss gutted me and forced my hand. I couldn't willingly continue to pursue every means possible to conceive and bear a child.

Devastated, I couldn't see my way clear to a purpose-filled, fruitful life if I wasn't going to have my own family.

You see, I always wanted to be a mom.

I mean, *always*.

It all began with a life-like baby doll Christmas present when I was two . . . I still have her.

She looked like a real baby and had a soft, weighted body that felt like an infant. I spent my early years playing with that doll and a variety of others.

My first "essay" written in #2 pencil on the Big Chief tablet and illustrated with blue sky and sienna told about my desire to grow up and become a nurse to take care of babies in the hospital nursery.

When I was eleven, I became an aunt for the first time.

Not too long after my niece was born, my mom put me on a Greyhound bus to visit my sister and her husband to help out with their new baby. When I arrived, my sister showed me the small day bed in my niece's nursery and taught me how to heat the baby's bottle and change her diaper.

Then she went to bed for two weeks.

(Well, that's how it seemed.)

I *was* the night nurse for the entire visit. I loved that sweet time of bonding with my niece. It served as a wonderful mom experience for me.

As I grew through teen years and into adulthood I never had to make the decision about whether or not I wanted to be a mom. It was never a question or an issue.

Through years of singleness I knew I was a mom who just hadn't had a baby yet. Over time, I gained more nieces and nephews, and I love them dearly. I thank God for the presence of these children (many now adults) in my life.

As a young adult, I was the single friend with children's books and Disney movies—collecting them for my future children. My friends who had kids knew I welcomed the chance to babysit and share the wonders of child-focused media.

I was thirty-eight when I finally began trying to start a family, and I had no clue that my age would be such a risk factor. The first pregnancy ended in a middle-of-the-night miscarriage soon after discovering the plus sign on the test stick. Those hours were some of the darkest and loneliest of my life.

That became the genesis of several years of tests, procedures, blood work, specialists, surgeries, and two more miscarriages. None of them led to my giving birth to a living child.

I did my very best to be fruitful and multiply. Healthy food choices, doctor visits, early morning daily temperature and charting, injections when necessary (and I *hate* needles), researching vitamins and treatments, and on and on . . . even acupuncture!

Did I mention I *hate* needles?

The physical side of things felt like a full-time, thankless job.

No babies.

I was devastated, and that led to a crisis of faith.

Don't get me wrong. I never doubted God's eternal salvation in Jesus Christ, but I was questioning God's provision and care of my life details, the desires of my heart. I knew my eternity was secure, but I wondered, did he care about my here and now?

Eternity someday, but does he care about my everyday here and now?

In the very beginning of human creation, we see God give Adam and Eve a mandate: "And God blessed them. And God said to them, 'Be fruitful and multiply and fill the earth and subdue it, and rule over the fish of the sea and over the birds of the sky and over every living thing that moves on the earth'" (Gen. 1:28).

Bearing a child.

Such a basic thing that women have done since the beginning of time, and yet, it was proving to be an impossible task for me.

The spiritual side felt overwhelming.

Unfortunately, in the sacred world we are told the stories of Sarah, Hannah, and Elizabeth in such a way that we believe they were blessed because God eventually gave them children. The summary of their situations: closed wombs, blessed by God, bore a child.

To those in emotional and spiritual pain, the implied message (many times directly spoken to the strugglers) often translates to, "If childbearing doesn't happen, we are cursed by God."

Thus continued the circle of questions I asked myself on a regular basis:

Did He care?

Really?

Was I not blessed by him?

What had I done wrong?

One of my friends from church sat across the dining room table one night trying to make sense of her situation. You see, she couldn't get pregnant.

We began discussing the whole blessings and curses issue (intended for a particular time and place), and she threw her Bible across the table and said, "So, am I cursed by God? Explain this to me!"

Over the course of the active infertility years in my life, crazy theology or beliefs about God came and went in my brain. Some of these were nonsensical conclusions of my own, and some were incorrect ideas implanted by others.

Friends, acquaintances, and strangers alike felt free to ask questions and give opinions: did I have any sin I hadn't prayed for forgiveness, had I prayed about generational curses in my family, etc. I could share for days about the "stories of encouragement." One much older person in my life (who has four children) told me how confusing he found my unwillingness to have children and questioned why I didn't have any.

In my momentary shock, I explained (in great pain) that I *was* trying and had recently suffered a second miscarriage.

His response?

"Well, I'll tell you. My wife was so fertile, all it took for her to get pregnant was for me to lay my pants on the end of the bed. Ha, ha, ha."

During the days of trial and trying, these attitudes and stories plunge like a knife into the heart and soul of someone struggling with infertility.

***

Lesson learned

Never let anyone press you for an explanation about private issues like this. If someone you don't know well crosses the boundary and asks/judges such a sensitive matter, you will only receive insensitive comments back should you choose to respond. If you feel discomfort, make a polite exit from the person and conversation.

***

In contrast, one of my oldest and dearest friends made this statement one day: "I don't get it. I don't understand your inability to get pregnant, stay pregnant, and have a child."

I responded, "That's okay. I don't get it either. I don't understand your ability to get pregnant, stay pregnant, and have children."

This might sound like she offered a blunt judgment; but really, I found it refreshing for someone to open a discussion in a loving way.

You see, I knew her heart was in the right place—she wasn't pressuring, questioning, assuming, etc. She honestly felt unable to comprehend my situation.

Through her willingness to step in, I felt welcomed to engage and inform her about some of my trials at the time.

You must have credibility in your relationship before initiating a delicate conversation like this. Be very careful with your assumption about what they want to hear from you.

By God's grace and through much prayer, Scripture, and wise counsel of others, I learned his truths and realized that he had a purpose for me.

The grief and bitterness took a long time to work through, and my confusion lived in the question of: *Why did God not allow any of my babies to enter this world?*

I struggled to understand my value and to determine what action could fill the purposeless void within. As a Christian woman seeking a kingdom-driven life under a "be fruitful and multiply" banner, how was I supposed to determine a way forward and not suffer permanent paralysis under the burden of the childlessness?

What production can serve as a substitute that fulfills the God-driven desire to create biologically?

Asking Key Questions

Have you ever sought something and missed seeing it right in front of you? Have you laughed at yourself after digging through a purse only to find the sunglasses you seek resting quietly on top of your head?

Or found yourself looking for the very telephone you were holding? (I've done that too—while telling the person on the other end about the struggle to find my phone!)

The Search

These little treasure hunts might make us laugh or cause brief irritation, but what happens when we desperately search for a new direction or purpose in life? Maybe the loss of a dream or a crushing emotional blow steers us away from what we sought towards something else.

But how do we find the *something else*?

Several years ago, I was quietly drowning in bitterness and despair during my quest to be a mom. The long process eventually made me face the inevitable, so I waved a white flag and put down the dream.

A cloud of confusion loomed over my life as I sought a new way to fully live out meaning and purpose. I found no map marked with "You Are Here" and a flag drawn over my life destination off in the distance.

I was lost, just putting one foot in front of the other. Plodding, really, with no direction or enthusiasm.

A Question

Then one day, an acquaintance approached me at church and posed a simple question:

Julie, I hear you play the piano, and we need a pianist at a retirement home church service. Would you be willing to play for us?

I could find no good reason to decline, and the day and time worked for me, so I said yes. (Oh, and I also envisioned my mother's face beaming with pride because those long-ago piano lessons and the tug-of-war over daily practice would finally serve a meaningful purpose.)

One question from someone I hardly knew led to a brand-new adventure with incredible people.

A new path.

And that new path led to another.

And another.

And another.

Suddenly, surprisingly, life purpose and dreams unfolded before me. I didn't recognize the gift one question could give. I didn't expect this question to lead down a fascinating trail and certainly didn't see it at the time.

Those black and white keys gave music to my world in more ways than one. They paved the way of hopeful expectation. I only now trace the twists and turns of the last several years back to the magnitude of that simple question:

Would you be willing to play for us?

Thank you, Ron, for asking.

Life seas have included the occasional storm: rough waves tossing me back and forth, gale force winds blowing me emotionally off course, and grief rains lashing my face. Faith, time, prayer, family, friends, and purpose have eased the raw pain.

I have learned that I will never "get over" not having children, but I can experience meaningful life as I learn to weave my past story into my future endeavors.

I struggled with life questions:

Who am I?
What do I do now?
How do I move forward?

Over time, two young relatives changed the course of my grief by posing identical questions.

They lived in two different states, and during two separate conversations these two pre-teen kids, who had witnessed my bitterness and pain by overhearing me discuss my infertility, asked me two questions:

Aren't I your child too?
Yes, of course you are!

Am I not enough?
Ouch.
Ouch.
Ouch.

My bitterness and grief over the loss of a life dream caused pain and questioning in the young lives of children who were and are dear to me. God used them to help get my attention. I needed to know he had wonderful loved ones present in my life and undiscovered purpose ahead of me.

The walls of isolation began to crack and the bars imprisoning my heart creaked open. Thus began a time of discovery that led to freedom in discovering God's plan for my life.

Twelve years later I ask myself the same life questions I asked during my active infertility season and found renewed promise and hope in the answers.

Who am I?
I am a child of God.

What do I do now?
Pay attention to what he puts before me
and seek to do his will.

How do I move forward?
By his grace, one step at a time.

The involuntarily childless woman who can answer the age-old question, "What am I doing here?" can find a lifeline to faith connection.

God created us for community.

Created in his image, we seek connection with others.

The practical compassion of community in the fallout of infertility and involuntary childlessness is vital.

It changed my life.

Do you have areas of bitterness and grief in your life? How do you process these emotions?

Do you have connection and community in the local church? If not, why not do some research and find one to visit?

Who in your life reaches out in heart relationship— someone with a listening, compassionate ear?

Chapter 2
What to Expect When
You're Not Expecting

Let me say up front:

I know the fear, and I get it. When I lived in the eye of the infertility storm, I only wanted to know about people with successful pregnancy/childbirth outcomes.

I refused to even consider the aftermath if I couldn't be a mom.

Maybe you fear an outcome like mine. It's okay. Truly.

Feel those feelings and own that you don't want to be like me and have your life turn out as mine did.

That said, I'm here to help.

I'm here to use my stomach-dropping, unbelievable, heart-lurching, stomach-rolling ball-of-awful to reach out a hand through words to encourage *you*.

To give voice to other women tumbled around by the swirl of infertility and childlessness.

Take what you need from our stories and situations, apply what you like, gather your peeps, cling to hope, and move forward.

Along the Way

The infertility crisis consists of five major components: physical, spiritual, emotional, relational, financial. No one's story is the same, but most will have challenges in these general areas.

Physical

After trying for a year to get pregnant, the strip barely registered the plus sign before I miscarried in the middle of the night.

Clueless about the combination of issues, I swallowed the tears and began again.

I had yet to realize that I had taken a sharp right turn off Happy Drive and headed into unexplored terrain.

There were no warning signs about steep trails or dangerous cliffs along the way. Even though I recall hearing how age affected pregnancy, I brushed it off as something I didn't need to worry about.

I needed someone to kindly look me straight in the eye and say, "You are thirty-eight years old. Trust me when I tell you your fertility will be a challenge. Do not *try* to get pregnant. Don't stress, but go straight to a well-respected fertility doctor or endocrinologist in your area and have them conduct basic tests."

You see, it was only much later that one of my doctors drew a simple chart showing the decline of a woman's fertility after age thirty-five. Not only is it more difficult to get pregnant, but the rate of successful deliveries also drops.

When I say drop, I mean the *heart-pounding-stomach-lurching-mind-spinning* drop of an amusement park ride.

Minus the amusement.

Whatever your age, I encourage you to consider adding this piece of information to your life journey supplies.

(*I have no medical training. I am just offering friendly advice from my experience and the experience of others who have walked this road.*)

If you are thirty, getting married, and want to have children, go see your doctor. Tell him or her that you don't want to waste time and would like basic bloodwork and tests to make sure you and your husband have no obvious challenges. There are simple ways to evaluate and address many issues.

If you are under thirty, getting married, and want to have children, relax! Enjoy time with your husband. I do advise friends in your age group who are actively trying to get pregnant to consider seeking basic medical advice after a year of no pregnancy.

Knowledge about your body and the role that age performs is foundational.

> **Knowledge about your body and the role that age performs is foundational.**

The warning signs may not obviously appear along our path, but once we experience roadblocks we can stay alert to what is happening in and around us and seek wise counsel from appropriate sources.

A Yolk of Reality

As women's reproductive options have opened up, so have medical technologies that assist in later pregnancies.

Looking at the "rise" or "fall" of fertility statistics is important, but ultimately foundational truth enables women to make informed decisions about their procreation future.

Female infants are born with ovaries containing their lifetime supply of eggs. As they age, so do their eggs, and there is a direct correlation between the effects of female aging and the ramifications on fertility and successful delivery.

In spite of medical assistance in reproduction, scientific facts related to age cannot be denied or discounted in the overall picture.

During the writing of this book, I've seen an increase in stories encouraging women to freeze their eggs to ensure future fertility and give them freedom in their current years. The unspoken understanding is that science will solve any future challenges.

May I offer a caution?

You must take the initiative, do the research, and seek advice from reliable sources about the realities of fertility. But if you reach the end of active fertility thinking that science alone will solve any issue that arises, understand that it is too late to turn back the clock. Age matters.

Science helps us achieve so much we are unable to accomplish alone. However, you need to stay informed on the realities of your personal situation.

Three occurrences I've observed lately spurred me to share with you.

1. During a local news story, a reporter provided information on freezing eggs for future fertility. I was

glad to see someone shine the light on this topic. She interviewed several young and middle adult women on why they chose to freeze their eggs or were planning to do so. I am all about options and utilizing science to our benefit, but one portion of her report troubled me. Her voiceover accompanied a graphic on age and fertility. She referred to the age of thirty-five, saying, "Women won't fall off the fertility cliff at age thirty-five but by forty, doctors say conceiving is harder. Science tells us younger eggs increase the chance of successful pregnancy and healthy babies."

According to numerous sources (and several doctors who advised me personally), there actually *is* a fertility cliff at age thirty-five. I sent a kind email to the news reporter expressing my concern that women have accurate sources and information about fertility and age.

I never received a response.

My dear younger sister in life, I want you to be *fully* informed.

2. Recently I viewed a story on a former Bachelorette (the reality show kind) who made headlines and warranted a short segment and interview on a national morning show due to her recent decision to freeze her eggs. The reporter for the story then showed a picture of other ex-Bachelorettes and several pictures of actresses who have done the same. The story also

presented statistics illustrating the growth in popularity of freezing eggs.

Again, anyone considering an intentional delay in childbearing must know all of the ramifications of age.

> 3. During a recent conversation with a newly married, over-thirty friend, we discussed this very topic. To paraphrase our conversation: She said she isn't too concerned because she heard that even though *they* used to believe that thirty-five was a fertility-challenged age, she heard *they* now believe it is really forty. I asked her who *they* were—I wanted to discover the source of information because I wanted to support her and make sure it was accurate and reliable. She had no idea who *they* were.

My goal is to empower you to self-advocate and learn the facts to help with your decision-making. Also, please be sure to research the egg retrieval procedure.

Understand the effects of aging on your body—young, frozen eggs will not always guarantee a successful pregnancy and healthy birth if there are underlying physical/health issues (and oftentimes these do exist, especially with age).

Words like freedom, empowerment, and peace of mind are used to describe opportunities to enlist the assistance of science and attempt to guarantee future fertility.

You Are Not Alone

A study through Harvard Health Publications explored an overall view of the infertility experience in the developing world. It concluded, "About five percent of couples living in the developed world experience primary infertility (inability to have any children) or secondary infertility (inability to conceive or carry a pregnancy to term following the birth of one or more children)."[11]

Studies show the psychological impact of infertility on men and women. The Harvard study "concluded that women with infertility felt as anxious or depressed as those diagnosed with cancer, hypertension, or recovering from a heart attack."[12]

Treatment for infertility can present physical and financial issues. Tests and procedures hold a dual challenge: the physical embarrassment and potential for shame, as well as the financial burden of tests, blood-work, surgeries, and procedures—most not covered by insurance. Underneath these obvious layers reside the subterranean levels of critical cultural and spiritual imprints on the infertility experience.

Numerous resources offer medical and physical details of the various aspects of infertility. The ASRM offers emotional information. For example, their website states:

> Infertility often creates one of the most distressing life
> crises that a couple has ever experienced together. The

long-term inability to conceive a child can evoke significant feelings of loss. Coping with the multitude of medical decisions and the uncertainties that infertility brings can create great emotional upheaval for most couples. If you find yourself feeling anxious, depressed, out of control, or isolated, you are not alone.[13]

The couple responding to infertility must understand that it's a puzzle of physical issues: sperm and egg health, implantation, fetal growth, and healthy delivery. The experience will also impact them emotionally.

Emotional

Richard Winter includes infertility in a discussion of life events and their connection to grief: "Sorrow and sadness invade our lives when we lose people or things that are precious and important to us. We usually think of grief in response to death, but we often experience some form of grief with other losses."[14]

Grief shows up with many negative life events. The same Harvard study also lists important experiences of the infertile person:

> Individuals who learn they are infertile often experience the normal but nevertheless distressing emotions common to those who are grieving any significant loss—

in this case the ability to procreate. Typical reactions include shock, grief, depression, anger, and frustration, as well as loss of self-esteem, self-confidence, and a sense of control over one's destiny.[15]

What seems to be a simple act of reproduction becomes, for the person in the midst of fertility challenges, a complicated mission.

You are not alone, and you haven't gone off a mental cliff! The emotions overwhelm. Chaos seems to reign. Sadness engulfs.

Infertility is a private matter, yet because of social media and immediate communication platforms, it garners public repercussions.

When you seek to have a child and so far have been unsuccessful, ideas on Pinterest for baby showers feel overwhelming. Baby celebrations and shower pictures on Instagram and Facebook provide feelings of inadequacy, and gender reveal videos bring sharp pangs of jealousy and fear.

These emotions may overwhelm you at different times in the journey and cause you to question God.

Spiritual

Often Christians suffer spiritual wounds through the bane of infertility and childlessness.

When something like giving birth, which seems so basic, is delayed or unachievable, spiritual challenges wreak soul-deep havoc that can haunt and overwhelm. Glahn and Cutrer detail the spiritual impact in *The Infertility Companion*. They write:

> Spiritual questions can cause the infertile couple more agony than the skyrocketing medical expenses, life on "hold," frustrating encounters at the physician's office, insurance hassles, and relational turmoil combined. In our dealings with thousands of infertility patients, only one said she never wondered if God might be punishing her. She was an atheist.[16]

Their insight speaks volumes about the Christian's spiritual dilemma in the midst of infertility and the need for an understanding church family.

For the Christian believer, the Bible is the instruction manual for life, and in its beginning pages we find the most fundamental life expectation. When a Christian is unable to bear a child, spiritual confusion ensues. Glahn and Cutrer elaborate on this key creation theme:

> As early as Genesis 1, we read that God told Adam and Eve to "be fruitful and multiply." We read it and think this is something we can and *must* do. It seems we are unable to do the very thing for which we were created. Weren't we created for procreation? That's how many people see God's command to the first couple to multiply—as a decree for all time.[17]

The authors explore this further and explain the difference between multiplying by physical means, human reproduction, in the Old Testament and the call for spiritual multiplication in the New Testament.

Believers are called to love God, love one another, and make disciples. The authors underscore the truth that "we are designed for more than human reproduction."[18]

I love this reminder from author Donna VanLiere of the truth of our lives, regardless of the labels we wear:

> When we read the words of Jesus to a lame man, "Do you want to be well?" our broken hearts and crippled spirits cry, "Yes! Yes! Yes!" And even though it's so much easier to keep dragging our baggage with us we work on getting rid of it, piece by painful piece.

> We know that we have lived and will continue to live a flawed and imperfect life but we also understand that the light of God can only get in through our cracks. This wisdom awakens in our soul the realization that there is a *Divine* plan for us. There is a Divine *plan* for us. There is a Divine plan *for* us. There is a Divine plan for *us*.[19]

Steps to Take

Wait Well

Waiting requires action. Action in the midst of infertility is difficult but necessary.

A *caveat*: if you are in the middle of raw grief over recent loss (miscarriage, stillbirth, child loss, or adult child passing), please proceed with care. What follows does not apply to you in this part of your timeline nor should it be used by friends or loved ones to "encourage" you and others to move on in your grief. Sometimes, for a time, you must sit in the puddles of life pain and just be, one breath at a time.

So many parts of the infertility puzzle require time and waiting.
- Waiting on the calendar
- Waiting on medications
- Waiting to see if you are pregnant
- Waiting to try again

In the midst of the passive waiting, wait well by taking action.

- Plan fun, non-fertility related activities and date nights with your husband. No fertility talk. Just go out and enjoy each other's company.

- Invite friends or family over for a fun game night.

- When appropriate, update your family members on your infertility journey.

  Only provide information you and your spouse have agreed to share with others and set loving, clear boundaries.

  For example, if you are in the middle of too many tests and procedures and don't have the energy or desire to share much, you might sit down with your parents and say, "We are in a struggle to get pregnant right now. It is a tough road and we are dealing with it the best we can. We would greatly appreciate your prayers, love, and support and will fill you in with news as we are able."

- As you decide to share your struggle, let those close to you know that you will need freedom, grace, and understanding about birthdays, family events, and holiday celebrations. Let them know you love them and their children and you might need to pass on attending some events. This can be tricky but it is an important part of your self-care. I once had a friend offer to buy a baby shower gift for me and take it to a baby shower because she knew I was not in a good emotional place to go. She even called in my RSVP. It was one of the most thoughtful actions anyone did for me during this time.

- Do you have another couple, with whom you are close and who are going through similar issues? Get together for dinner, Bible study, talk about the ins and outs of infertility that no one else may understand or want to hear. This might be a good way to process as couples and gain a better understanding of the opposite sex's unique way of approaching all that is happening.

- Another couple can be supportive and present in waiting rooms during surgeries or procedures or to hang out with when you want to just "be" and not explain moods, sadness, etc.

- Recruit a close friend or two to support and encourage you and even hold you accountable. By this, I mean, someone you trust to be empathetic when necessary and also to give a little tough love when you are in isolation and distress. This requires great trust and participation.

- Be ready to offer great amounts of grace. People will not know what to do or how to help, and they may say hurtful things. Assume they mean the best for you and that they just don't know.

When people haven't been through a similar circumstance they might not be capable of offering what you specifically need, and that requires a deep breath, patience, and a large helping of grace!

Stay Aware of Upcoming Events

Infertility, which includes miscarriage, is a topic many people do not openly discuss.

Different seasons and large events bring particular aches for the mom hollow within. One of the toughest is Mother's Day.

Advertisements remind us to call, write, send a card, or board an airplane to act on our love for Mother's Day.

What can we do when the thought of Mother's Day makes our hearts twist and our stomachs lurch?

1. Acknowledge

We can't run from the pain in our lives. We might try to bury it deep within but it will rise up one day and won't be pretty. Pain, anger, and bitterness are best examined in the light of truth and love, faced head-on (as you are able), and walked through at your own pace. Ask trusted friends or relatives for their support and presence. Depending on the depth and severity you may need the help of a professional counselor to walk with you through the process.

2. Remember

Spend time reflecting on women who had a loving impact on your life. Make a list of those who have shown up, cared, and encouraged you on your journey. Call them or send a handwritten note (the flow of ink on paper stimulates the flow of memories) thanking them for specific, positive ways they influenced your life.

3. Reach Out

Review your list of women who showed care for you. What did they do to show their love? What are specific examples of how they encouraged you? What have you seen women do for others through positive interactions in life, movies, or books?

Write down these inspiring acts. Then make a separate list of people in your family, neighborhood, and workplace who need to know that kind of nurturing care and encouragement. Reach out to them and pass it on.

I am thankful for the gift of my mother—she is a loving example of care and nurture and demonstrates the beauty of a well-lived life.

Transform

Let's acknowledge our pain, remember the women who nurtured us, and reach out to those who need love! In the process, may we find our own Mother's Day transformed from ashes and mourning to beauty and joy!

If not . . . if you are weary, not only of the not-yet pain but also the inability to move, I encourage you to take your first step through the Mother's Day obstacle. Will you choose to move offensively this year by reaching *out* for what you can do for yourself instead of waiting for others to reach in?

So often I hear people express concern and uncertainty on what to do for you, their friend, their co-worker, their loved one. They fear saying or doing the wrong thing and end up doing nothing, which can lead to feelings of isolation and misunderstanding.

One way to alleviate this confusion is for you and me to reach out through this obstacle course of life and begin to move through. Shaky steps they may be, but once a step is in motion a way opens up for strength to seep its way through our being.

Plan

Make a plan for Mother's Day weekend—call someone for lunch or dinner and a movie. Ask a friend on a nature walk and talk about ways you feel thankful in life and use this time to thank God for what you *do* have.

Reach out to someone who was a mothering influence in your life—your own mother, a relative, former teacher, aunt, cousin, or a neighbor who spoke life into your younger child-self. Send a note or make a phone call and give them the gift of appreciation for ways their lives had positive impact. They probably have no idea the gift of their presence in a season of your life.

Above all else, *trust.*

When you can't see a way through the fog of disappointment and bitterness, *trust.*

When you feel so lost, you feel like a toddler again, *trust.*

When you grow weary of the physical humiliation of tests and poking and prodding, *trust.*

When you are terrified to look at the toilet paper, *trust*.

When you suffer a new wave of mourning every twenty-eight days, *trust*.

The times a friend, family member, church member, co-worker, or medical person says or does something so appallingly inappropriate, *trust*.

As you look at the mountain you have to climb, and have no idea what your life looks like on the other side, *trust*.

Trust in the one who lovingly created you. Know that he has wonderful plans for your life in spite of what you see right in front of you. Faith is trusting—it is not knowing what comes next but relying on the one who holds you in the palm of his hand. Trust is a verb and requires a lot of energy, time, and practice.

You can do it.

 Plan a special dinner with your spouse. Discuss finding another couple you both trust and can ask to walk with you through this season.

Set an appointment for you and your spouse to meet with your doctor and discuss overall treatment/game plan.

Find a Bible verse that gives you comfort and hope. Read it every day.

If you would like more helpful guidance and tools for the infertility experience, please see the additional resource I wrote: *Infertility & Involuntary Childlessness: Traveling the Terrain.*

Chapter 3
Vacancy Sign

Once, a neighbor showed me a nest filled with eggshell fragments. Two days later I spotted tiny goslings and two adults on the water.

Over several weeks I watched the goslings grow until they became young adults.

I began daily to seek the family of five and count their gaggle. It took me a while to discover why I was so drawn to them. Then one day it hit me.

They symbolized my own "would-be" family.

I guess the geese became a sweet reminder about my five-member family that never came to be after my three miscarriages and years in the middle of infertility. It has been over a decade since I stopped actively pursuing a family and came to the end of the motherhood dream I dreamed for a lifetime.

Over the years I grieved on many levels, worked through disappointment and bitterness, and learned to grab onto new life pursuits.

Wherever you find yourself on the childless journey, I want to encourage you: You are not alone in your travels.

There are many who have wandered the roads of grief and loss. I implore you to reach out to someone who has been there, who can offer a listening ear.

Invite trusted friends and loved ones into your walk. Ask them to just be there. They don't need to offer explanations or advice, just be a caring presence to shoulder the burden.

Take your time on this road. There is no set timeline for grief—everyone's experience is unique. The important thing to remember is to *step forward.*

Maybe you take a *big* step.

Maybe a *small* one.

You might step off the path for a longer *rest stop.*

You might take several steps *backward.* That's okay.
Engage *forward* motion again. And don't stay too long in isolation.

Pray.

I'll be praying for you—for comfort, strength, and hope.

We need one another.

We need a gaggle to call our own—those cherished people who paddle alongside through the sun-glistened waters of life.

Cultural Impact

The life of a childless woman morphs into a life of not fitting in with the twenty-first century Western way of life. For women who wanted to bear children and could not, they do not completely fit in with their single friends, married friends with children, friends who successfully overcame infertility issues, and friends who consider themselves (completely) childfree (never wanted to have children). Justine Froelker offers a glimpse into her personal journey:

> Now, as an adult woman without children, I'm struggling, for the first time in my life, with a sense of not belonging. By the classic and most widely accepted definition of a woman my age, I will never fit in. I am not a mother. I am constantly reminded of this; in the congregation full of families, in the group of moms discussing feeding or soccer schedules, in the childfree by choice group (some of which don't even necessarily like kids) or on Facebook walls which are filled with pictures of birthdays, the first day of school and the holiday Elf on a Shelf fun.[20]

The combination of pain from unfulfilled childbearing dreams with a new reality of ill-fitting characteristics requires recovery, healing, and an intentional reframing of life.

Once a couple decides to lay down the dream of having children and move forward, they must consider not only the emotional impact but also the cultural. Their identity in infertility changes within themselves, yet they are still adrift.

Women, who once provided support, encouragement, and lament, now gather to exclaim over the daily joys and trials of newfound motherhood. The childless couple must move into a new area in culture, alongside fellow travelers whose dreams came true and through an uncertainty world that seems to set a motherhood expectation.

Pamela Mahoney Tsigdinos shares her story on the decision she and her husband made to "loosen their grip on their fragile dream" and move forward: "We're expelled and left to find our way back to some kind of normal within a society that celebrates motherhood, and we're surrounded by parents preoccupied with childrearing—at work, on newsstands, on TV, and on the Internet."[21]

Daily interactions and reminders provide no evident way to resolve the grief and pain that accompanies the loss of dreams and life. Kathe Wunnenberg details the grief conundrum found in pregnancy loss:

Many people—family, friends, neighbors, coworkers, and the community—feel the trauma and tragedy of the death of adults and young lives. Obituaries validate their existence. But with a pregnancy loss, there are few memories, and the ones that exist live only for the woman and perhaps her husband. How are we to grieve someone society does not expect us to grieve?[22]

The validation of the specific loss (pregnancy or infant) as well as the loss of the motherhood dream is vital for the couple to move through a healthy season of grief. This allows them to move into a new, fruitful life holding their loss as an important part of their reality without staying stuck in the depths of despair.

Generational Trends

Melanie Notkin examines the experience of women who are childless, particularly those who remain so due to their single status:

"The rise of childless women may be one of the most overlooked and underappreciated social issues of our time. Never before have so many women lived longer before having their first child or remained childless toward the end of their fertility."[23]

The delay in childbearing brings huge ramifications for future fertility and reproduction. The ASRM presents age-related statistics and the resulting impact on fertility:

Fertility gradually declines in the 30s, particularly after age 35. Each month that she tries, a healthy, fertile 30-year-old woman has a 20% chance of getting pregnant. That means that for every 100 fertile 30-year-old women trying to get pregnant in 1 cycle, 20 will be successful and the other 80 will have to try again. By age 40, a woman's chance is less than 5% per cycle, so fewer than 5 out of every 100 women are expected to be successful each month.[24]

Childlessness has the potential to grow in proportion with the large number of women delaying, intentionally or not, pregnancy and childbirth. The populated group of childlessness will also be affected by the aging Baby Boomer generation, empty nesters whose lifestyles now encompass a form of childlessness.

Journalist Travis Andrews compares the Baby Boomer generation to the influential millennial generation:

Pew Research Center broke down population estimates released this month by the U.S. Census Bureau. For this exercise, the millennial generation included anyone who was 18 to 34 years old in 2015. Therefore, the oldest Millennial (sic) was born in 1981 and the youngest in 1997. By that definition, there are now 75.4 million living Millennials (sic), which is a half-million more than the 74.9 million living baby boomers, who were defined as anyone who was 51 to 69 years old in 2015.[25]

The church and her members often increase spiritual maladies for the infertile. Resorting to clichés, inappropriate "church speak," untimely Scripture quotation, and the stressful seeking of a quick answer to pain leads to misrepresentation (at best) and a contribution to further isolation and pain for the couple (at worst).

Glahn and Cutrer offer a caution when invoking biblical answers to questions from the infertile. They write, "The Bible provides many relevant answers to questions the average infertility patient asks. Unfortunately, some teachers and writers have distorted its message in such a way that it inflicts even more suffering on those enduring the pain of childlessness."[26]

A focus on life in the God-honoring sense is a focus on life lived for him and to his glory. Many believe this is best lived by producing a family; however, every person is a unique creation of God, made in his image for his purpose and will. Hubbard emphasizes this quest for life in a study of Deuteronomy 30:19:

> The challenge to choose life was relationally based, emphasized in every aspect of the renewed covenant. Choose life, God urged them, and in urging this choice, God clearly intended life to be more than physical survival. God wanted them to choose rich, full, productive life in relationship with Him, life as He intended it to be. But this choice was not a one-time event—it was a process of choosing.[27]

Whether infertile or fertile, childfree, childfull, or childless, the life of a believer is rooted in God through Christ Jesus. Drawing close in relationship with God is a daily exercise on the part of the believer.

Fruitful Living

Our lives become more intentional when we know our gifts, purpose, and identity. Every Christian possesses the foundational purpose to love God, love others, proclaim Jesus, and know their true identity as a child of the King. This is imperative for the assurance of the human role in the overarching story of God's redemption.

Scripture illustrates the truth that child production is not the only path to a godly, fruitful life in Jesus. Many people, including Christians, place the notion of success or failure in life on their ability to have children. Desperation can ensue until nothing matters but the gain found in having a child.

Identity

One way to experience transformation in living with infertility is a renewed understanding of identity. Labels obtained and responsibilities performed are not a person's identity. They are descriptives of life positions and activities.

A Christian's root identity is found in knowing and belonging to the Lord.

We must first and foremost love and serve God. Messages from the Christian subculture must communicate this truth clearly without a motherhood expectation that adds pressure and heartache.

An understanding of true identity provides the key building block for a woman who seeks the title of "mom." Western culture has a tendency to condition people to claim their roles, vocations, and titles as their identity. Yet Christians must root their identity in Christ Jesus first, because everything else fails and falls away. In the words of the Apostle Paul,

> He [Christ] is the image of the invisible God, the firstborn of all creation. For by him all things were created, both in the heavens and on earth, visible and invisible, whether thrones or dominions or rulers or authorities—all things have been created through him and for him. He is before all things, and in him all things hold together. He is also head of the body, the church; and he is the beginning, the firstborn from the dead, so that he himself will come to have first place in everything. For it was the Father's good pleasure for all the fullness to dwell in him, and through him to reconcile all things to himself, having made peace through the blood of his cross; through him, I say, whether things on earth or things in heaven (Col. 1:15–20).

Christ created all things. As creator, sustainer, and redeemer, he is the source of meaning and life. This realization and foundational knowledge equips men and women to find their identity first in him.

If identity is dependent on bearing a child and being a mom, then those who are unable to bear children could face the inability to move forward into fruitful living, because they might feel they lacked identity.

Testimonies

Each woman interviewed for this research recognized that she is a child of God and a co-heir with Jesus Christ, and her core identity is in Christ, even though each one spent a period of time wrestling with competing labels.

Francine described her ultimate conclusion this way: "I am God's child to do whatever work he wants to do for whatever reason in my life."

Lois described her struggle with the reconciliation that she would not be a mom. She said, "I always thought I'd be a mom." Then she wrestled with her biblical understanding of Almighty God and his love and creation of her. She concluded, "*Imago Dei*—I'm created in the image of God, fully, with or without children."

René presented her struggle and ultimate understanding of her definition: "I am not defined by family, work, or interests. I am defined as a beautiful child of God. If I'm not careful, I can suffer from identity theft."[28]

Once women understood their true identity, what they were called to do, and which gifts they were given, their strategies and understandings of what it means to have a life of meaning were transformed.

Such understanding did not provide overnight healing and comprehension of events. But as they moved through the process of healthy grieving and became more informed about God's true plan, they began to discover new ways of thinking and acting on God's truth for their lives.

On her New Life website, Margaret Mowczko asks,

> What about those people who do not have a family? When churches make marriage and motherhood the pinnacle and priority of Christian womanhood, women who remain unmarried or childless may view themselves as lonely failures. Churches need to make efforts to ensure that single or childless men and women feel welcome, included and valued in church communities.[29]

Titus 2 instruction gives meaning and purpose in women's lives within the church family.

Author Staci Eldredge explores the meaning of the verb *mother*:

All women are not mothers, but all women are called *to mother.* To mother is to nurture, to train, to educate, to rear. As daughters of Eve, all women are uniquely gifted to help others in their lives become more of who they truly are—*to encourage, nurture, and mother them toward their true selves.* In doing this, women partner with Christ in the vital mission of bringing forth life.[30]

Spiritual mothering is sacred work and can result in bearing fruit and multiplying God's love outside the nuclear family.

Purpose

In *Finding Grace,* VanLiere describes a movie scene that inspired her to seek purpose beyond her pain.

Chariots of Fire tells the story of Eric Liddell, Olympic gold medal winner from the 1924 Olympics. In the film, he explains his calling: "I know God made me for a purpose. For China. But he also made me fast. And when I run I feel his pleasure."

VanLiere recalls, "'When I run I feel his pleasure.' These seven words popped off the screen in bold, emotional color. They were affecting and piercing because I didn't know what that was like, to enjoy doing something so much that it felt as if the Creator himself was smiling when I did it. That simple line reflected my own interior wanderings and my desperation to know what on earth I was here for."[31]

Almighty God has a purpose for every human life. Women living through infertility and childlessness tire of biblical stories with a redemption theme that rests on fruitful childbearing.

Common emphasis on these stories brings forth not only frustration but also a predicament of pain and withdrawal from God and his people.

Authors Glahn and Cutrer offer a clarifying thought on fertility: "The Bible's infertility narratives were not written to teach principles about facing infertility per se. Yet they can provide much insight into the struggle of infertility and how God views it."[32] The authors provide clarity for persons searching the biblical text for a literal answer to their infertility dilemma.

When the reality of childlessness sets in, stories of biblical childlessness can offer hope.

Glahn and Cutrer provide specifics: "We find within the pages of Scripture some couples who had no children. If Priscilla and Aquila had kids, they go without mention. And the prophetess and judge Deborah appears to have had no children, yet she was called 'a mother in Israel' (Judg. 5:7)."[33]

Glahn and Cutrer offer a poignant view and ask a raw question with regard to the gift of children: "The Bible says, 'Children are a gift from the Lord; the fruit of the womb is His reward' (Ps. 127:3). Does that mean I don't qualify?"[34] The authors describe the ultimate gift of salvation that is enough for all. Then they offer, "God blesses all of His children, but He chooses to distribute specific gifts differently. These gifts are not limited to children, nor are babies His 'ultimate' gift."[35]

When encouraging others to use their gifts and talents in the midst of loss and reality, the would-be encourager must take care with regard to time and place.

How Women Found True Value and Meaning in Life

Isolation, worry about the future, and exclusion are but a few concerns of the childless woman in the church. Involvement with others and the use of individual gifts and talents could not replace the grief and trials of childlessness but could meet the need for purpose and fruitfulness.

In the discussion of her infertility journey, Elizabeth emphasized the influence of people who led her to discover and understand her gifts and talents. She offered advice about finding meaning and value: "I sought ways to serve. It is important to make yourself available."

Women looking for value in the middle of life circumstances must be willing to grow in awareness about their gifts and talents and seek ways to serve in their church community. The timeframe of action depends on each person's grief, personality, and outcome of the specific situation.

What the Involuntarily Childless Can Do

- Communicate, to the degree you are comfortable, with your relatives, friends, and church family. They cannot reach out in support if they do not know you are in need. Julia offered this encouragement: "Don't be afraid to ask for what you need."

- Pursue close relationships with women who will offer patience, grace, and loving support. Encourage them to allow you room to mourn and grieve and also truthfully and lovingly encourage you to engage in life again when the timing is appropriate for *you*.

- Pay attention to what God puts before you, to the needs around you, to the passion of your heart.

- Have hope. When asked what she wished others knew about her infertility experience, Jennifer shared this important exhortation: "There's wonderful, rich, happy, fulfilling, joy-filled life on the other side!" Julia shared her optimism as well: "I'm okay with it. I've learned to see the joy through it. Don't live in the *what if,* because God's plan is better."

- Allow yourself a timeframe of isolation, if necessary, and remember to eventually reach out to others. Savannah advised, "We're not alone. We need to talk."

Keep perspective about the entirety of life as your individual grief and journey allow.

René encouraged with, "Infertility was just an experience, a very small part of my life ordered by God. He had something marvelous in store for me. God loves us and carries us through. We have to allow him to."

Elizabeth shared her years of fruitful living through the lens of an eternal perspective: "I've had a life of blessing. Learn to look at life through a grid from his viewpoint versus the world's viewpoint. Study his Word to know what he thinks, and make a choice to live for him (I'm not perfect in this)."

The disappointment, confusion, and frustration with God during the journey through infertility and childlessness can be a stark reality. Time, wise counsel, prayer, study of Scripture, community support, and realization of God's faithfulness play key roles in an individual's willingness to walk toward new fulfillment and opportunities.

The timeframe and manner in which the interviewees accepted childlessness differed for everyone.

No grief walk is the same.

At an appropriate time, those without children must be willing to abandon their isolation in order to bravely reach into their faith community and offer their gifts, talents, and love.

Many are hesitant to engage in the surrounding culture because they fear facing standard small talk. For example, ice-breaking questions usually include some form of, "How many children do you have?" and most groups of women have a variety of "I have _____ children" in their introduction.

These everyday situations create havoc inside the woman who said goodbye to her mom dream. When you are ready, developing standard answers to commonly asked social questions can help you prepare to meet social situations and settings.

Missy shared how she learned to engage deeper conversations when meeting new people: "When I meet someone I say, 'Tell me about you.' Who is this person? This changed the shape of how to meet and get to know people."

René answered questions about children with healthy deflection: "That was not God's will for my life and he's given me _____ or I don't have any children but I have been blessed by doors opening to other things I would do. Redirect and deflect."

Elizabeth had a lifetime of answering questions about children. She answered, "'None.' I don't fiddle with it. This is not something that I want to give any more information than I have to, and I hope they can accept that."

Over varying lengths of time, these women have experienced positive and negative encounters and words through their cultures and communities. Hopefully the knowledge of their experiences will lead to better understanding and practical compassion.

Inhaling deeply, I stepped on the swinging tire that hung above the water. The hole in the middle appeared huge and the tire rim that was my step target looked thin and inadequate.

That first step overwhelmed my being.

Then I heard my nephew calling encouragement from behind. "You can do this, Aunt Julie. Just step on the tire and don't look down. You can do this."

When circumstances and seasons of the year overwhelm with pain, confusion and fear cause us to turn every direction searching for a sure step.

Living in the fresh thickness of depression can seem hopeless. For those of you further along the way of grief and disappointment, may I ask you to try something?

You see, I know well the timid, fearful anticipation of gasping internal reminders of not only loss, but also the reality of never-to-be, life-giving childbirth.

It stinks.

Enough time has passed that I have experienced the emotional spectrum and have spent time building what life can be in this ongoing new reality. Maybe you have as well.

Take a deep breath.

Take a step.

I'm encouraging you from behind.

"You can do this! Reach out. Take a step. Begin to move through."

The first step I took on the swinging tire (one of several tires) scared me but I had a loved one behind me encouraging me the whole way. I made it through that entire obstacle course above the pool and then did a second round.

It was exhilarating, and I felt a sense of accomplishment.
I pray that you will step out, reach out to someone close in your life today.

Take a baby step toward positive action in your reality.

You can do this.

Plan a special dinner with your spouse. Discuss finding a trustworthy couple to walk together through this season.

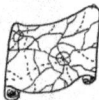

Review your treasured memories. Write down names and specifics to relive happy times.

Remember that your experience is yours to move through; grieve in your own way. Take time to think about the future reality of living re-engaged with healthy space for your heartache.

Chapter 4
Practical Compassion
In Community

Shortly after my second miscarriage I had an encounter with two older male relatives whom I rarely saw and who had no idea about my struggle to have a baby. Our conversation barely began when one of them asked me, "*Why, after a few years of marriage, don't you have any children?*"

He quickly moved into, "*I don't understand you young women who wait to have children; what is wrong with you?*"

Tears immediately welled in my eyes, then a wave of righteous indignation swept over me. How dare he assume things about my life. He had no idea what I was going through.

Both men continued discussing my life until I finally could stand no more and blurted out, "You have *no* idea what is going on in my life. For your information I just had my second miscarriage!"

The roar of crickets followed.

I knew they both cared for me and wanted the best for me, and they were uncomfortable with my sad news; however, pain and humiliation overwhelmed me.

My goal in this chapter is not to make you feel guilty if you have said something similar to a friend or loved one. I seek to help readers understand how our responses affect those in infertility and childlessness.

Your words matter. Start right now and commit to being more sensitive to hurting people around you. Be silent if you don't know what to say, or offer positive words and actions.

Community

Laurie Lisle shares the need for community:

> In our era, when so many nulliparas [nonmothers by author's definition] live alone or among unknown neighbors in large cities, most of us feel a strong need for community. It can be a desire for a communion of the spirit or psyche, in which communication takes place by long-distance telephone or even by computer, or for an actual neighborhood or town in which to relate to others.[36]

The desire for community experienced by unbelievers and believers alike is God-given and God-desired for his church.

Western Culture

Emily discussed the cultural expectation of motherhood and home by sharing her everyday struggle with feelings of inadequacy. She also described the pain that still surfaces when she sees social media pictures of her friends' children. She gained strength by listening to songs like "I Trust in You" by Lauren Daigle.

Lois told the opposite story by sharing that she did not feel less valued by Western culture community. Her best friend from Africa was barren, too, and people in that culture were less accepting of such a reality. Through hearing her experience, Lois realized Western culture and community actually valued her in spite of her inability to have children.

Several women talked in their interviews about challenges they experienced in Western culture. They are typically asked in social settings, "How many children do you have?"

Children are an expected, almost assumed, fact of life—especially in suburban America. Often the answer of "I do not have any children" halts the conversation.

René experienced this and said, "It *never* goes away." Often people follow up the question with, "Why not?" She described the judgment felt when asked, "Why not?" by a total stranger and explained that she and her husband prepared answers ahead of time to respond to a variety of questions. This helped them avoid extreme feelings of discomfort and surprise in public.

Childbirth is common for much of the population, and in many all-female social situations, introductions include sharing information about children. The involuntarily childless woman can experience feelings of inadequacy when describing her life that includes only children of the four-legged variety.

The lack of having children is felt in other contexts as well. Julia described the media onslaught of advertising for moms: Mother's Day, baby products, toys, shopping, and Disney World. She described having difficulty when people in the church community have no understanding of her childless pain reality. She said, "Society is hard; church is harder."

Lois explained her feelings of loss in a church environment. She desires to pass on her Christian faith and heritage to the next generation, just not in the way she dreamed of long ago.

Of all the interviewees, Elizabeth was the furthest from her years of active infertility, and she explained that the grandmother season is harder than her original time of seeking motherhood: "All of the women my age talk about their grandchildren."

As life-seasons change and women age, activity levels adjust and become slower. Women whose children are grown look forward to visits from children and grandchildren, which become a large focus of their lives. For older women with no children, the grandchildren season can be difficult.

Several of the interviewees discussed the surprise of discovering a renewed time of mourning their childlessness.

Savannah poured her energy into her career because society offers validation and meaning, and she did not receive this from her church peers. Several of the women mentioned their work and its provision of surface-level meaning for certain times of their life.

In spite of such meaning derived from work, Francine shared the deeper level of family: "So much emphasis on marriage and kids . . . A lot of value is placed on family. I felt lesser; I felt less. Certain times of the year are especially hard."

The women understood that mainstream Western culture has an expectation of marriage and children. Several of the women expressed genuine concern about who will care for them as they age.

How we can help

Many people in the middle of the infertility journey feel all alone. As a society we don't give many words to this topic and infertile couples often sit in isolation. Here are a few suggestions on how we can help:

1. Reassure your loved ones that they are not alone.
2. Offer a listening ear. (Be sure of your willingness to hear things like the opening story before you offer.)

3. Ask to accompany them to medical appointments if your friend's spouse is unable to go along. Knowing someone who has your best interest at heart sits a few feet away provides wonderful assurance. If the visit involves an office consultation it helps to have an objective set of ears (only if they welcome your presence in the meeting).

4. Stand ready to be present. Shrug off feelings of rejection if they do not accept your offer. There are many layers of emotion attached to this excursion called infertility and we must all be reminded not to allow any of the emotion to affect our relationship and care for one another.

5. Show up and quietly sit with the spouse while they occupy the surgical waiting room. Just being present is huge. It can be so lonely and fearful waiting on the one you love.

Your quiet presence speaks volumes. Many who have never been through this experience might make remarks to their loved ones about their "obsession" or "health issues."

Consider this scenario that might help clarify a situation like this.

A friend of mine, let's call her Mary, wanted more than anything to conceive and bear a child. She suffered through several years of infertility and the resulting tests, blood work, monitoring, and surgeries. Her medical team tried everything. During the process of trying to get pregnant, Mary's days revolved around doing all that the medical plan required.

One day, a friend looked Mary in the eye and accused her of obsession with having a child. I guess this friend didn't take time to ask or talk but just felt fed up with hearing Mary lament her predicament.

> *All I hear about is your trying to get pregnant . . . Every time we talk.*

> *Can't you focus on anything else in life? You just need to stop focusing on having a baby. You think about it too much.*

Mary, feeling misunderstood and defeated, responded.

> *Maybe I can only talk about my struggle to get pregnant because that is my focus right now. Of course I think about it all the time. Every day when I wake up I must take my temperature and write it on a chart before my feet even hit the ground. If I forget and move around before taking my temperature it ruins that morning's tracking. Temperature monitoring is key to knowing what my body is doing. I then head to the bathroom and meet my husband where he gives me my daily shot. The rest of the day is spent paying attention to what I do and eat. Each day the schedule begins again.*

Clichés and Advice

Please, please, do your best to avoid clichés. They are usually not helpful.

Sometimes when I am faced with a person in a difficult situation I want to have an answer or offer up something that will make *me* feel better. But the goal here is not to make *ourselves* feel better, but to offer care and community to *them* in *their* time of need. Even if you haven't been through this situation you can still be present and be a companion and supporter.

It is okay not to have an answer!

Please refrain from offering too much advice. Ask what you can do to help.

Offer to research or gather helpful information but if they don't take you up on your offer, don't be offended and keep newfound knowledge to yourself until asked.

There might be a time when your loved ones don't share what is happening in their life, and that is hurtful. I know it can feel alienating and painful, but remember this is about the person we're trying to help. We need to practically offer presence and support *they* need during each phase of this time.

It is okay
to not have the answer.

Questions

When you haven't traveled this road you don't realize how questions can sting.

Many couples are so busy discerning their infertility situation through a haze of rawness that they don't walk around sharing about being in the middle of this trauma. So while they are desperately trying to bring a child into this world, people around them might wonder why they don't have children yet.

My advice? Ask child questions with great care, *if at all*.

Once a couple has confirmation of infertility, just running an errand can be painful. Stores can be filled with strollers and moms during particular times of the day. If you have not fought in the infertility trenches you might be inclined to say, "Why can't they just get over it?"

If you haven't walked in their shoes you might not understand or sympathize. Please refrain from ever saying, "Get over it."

Fear

Every day can be a new exercise in fear management for a woman who has previously miscarried. Any unusual cramp can spark a twinge of nervousness.

For a long time I was afraid to go to the bathroom. I never wanted to experience the sight of blood on toilet paper again. Bleeding was a first sign for me that something was wrong.

Every twenty-eight days is a roller coaster for couples in infertility. It is an ongoing battle of emotions—fear, hope, defeat, and mourning. After a negative sign on the pregnancy test stick, the emotional cycle begins again, hand-in-hand with the physical cycle.

Every twenty-eight days is a new start that can lead to fresh disappointment.

Giving your friend or loved one a positive nugget of support each day will be appreciated. Calendars are not an infertile couple's friend. Daily reminders of your love and support can help counter their daily disappointments.

Relational

Several years ago in the midst of my struggle, a friend called me with the following offer:

> *Julie, I know that you were invited to Kate's baby shower, and I know you are facing a fierce struggle and might not want to attend. I am headed to the baby store after work tonight and would love to pick out a gift on her registry, wrap it, and take it to the baby shower for you. How much would you like me to spend on the gift?*

Crazy—writing this story still brings tears to my eyes.

That was one of the most loving acts I have ever experienced. I didn't have any desire to attend that particular baby shower. My pain was fresh and I did not want to celebrate someone else's pregnancy at that point in time—and this friend got it!

Not only did she understand, but she also called with a solution. I well remember this very matter-of-fact conversation that ended with me in tears of gratitude and feeling a one-ton boulder fall from my shoulders.

Often, couples have suffered a miscarriage (others may or may not know) and a family member or a friend is having a baby shower or toddler's birthday party.

Family and friends expect them to attend, but couples in the struggle may not feel up to it. This has nothing to do with the child being celebrated and is not a reflection of their love. This space overflows with pain and questions about them and their situation.

They might look at this event and think, "Will we ever have a baby shower?" "We can't even get pregnant." "They started trying after we did and now they are able to celebrate the upcoming birth of their child." Or when a child's birthday party is at hand they may wonder if they will ever have the opportunity to plan their two-year-old's party.

Please, if this situation occurs in your life, offer grace and an excused absence to that couple.

Financial

A dear friend who experienced years of infertility offered me a brilliant piece of advice. Because I knew about her experience, I called after my first miscarriage, seeking her input and guidance.

She said, "The very first thing you and your spouse need to do is draw your financial line in the sand. You don't realize it now but the further you go on this journey the more emotions are involved and the more money you will throw at the situation as you are presented with costly options. Sit down together tonight and determine a dollar amount you are willing to commit and stick to it."

Everything was costly and nothing was covered by insurance, not even basic tests and blood work (one vital blood test alone was $900). For some periods of time I had weekly sonograms, and those were not cheap. Spousal agreement is necessary for all of the decisions and costs.

Finances in marriage are tricky in the best of times, but during the stress of infertility treatment and exploration expenses quickly skyrocket and "possible" solutions can cause spending to spiral out of control.

Meaning and Involvement

A childless woman may find meaning and fruitfulness through involvement in mentoring and other areas of influence, both inside and outside of the church community.

In *The Body Project*, Joan Jacobs Brumberg examines the experience of young girls in America. She addresses the ways culture, society, the medical community, and changes in societal structure influence females.

Ads and marketing messages surround young women, influencing them to live autonomous lives. The conclusion of Brumberg's research shows that such messages emphasize living in a way that does not include others, out of the confines of true community.

Brumberg offers a study of girls in decades past who were surrounded by other women in community—aunts, neighbors, teachers—who took an interest in guiding them.[37]

Now, as then, there are avenues through which the church and community can provide opportunities for adult women with no children to impart wisdom and healthy friendship to teens and young women.

Invite your friend or family member to participate in life with you! If you have children, include her (and her husband) in family events like school programs or just have them over for dinner.

(**Caveat:** Always offer grace if they are not in an emotional place to participate. Ask with care and freedom for them to join in or take a raincheck!)

Supportive Action and Love

What *To* Do

- During medical tests, surgeries, and miscarriage, reach out with love and encouragement through meals or notes.
- Take your friend to a non-child atmosphere: spa treatment, museum; or engage in volunteer work to help someone else in need.
- Don't walk on eggshells; be open with your friend and offer your support and a listening ear.
- Understand and offer grace for emotional rawness.
- Get outside with your friend for a walk but avoid popular parks and places for moms and strollers.
- Write "I'm thinking of you notes." Be brief. Better too few words than offering stories or advice that just create more emotional pain.
- Bring laughter with you! Funny movie, comedy show, etc. Know material/subject matter before you present it! Laughter lifts the spirits!

What *Not* to Do

- Avoid these stories—"My brother's wife's best friend's mom's aunt's daughter went through the same thing and . . ."
- Don't share your own or other's stories of fertility success.
- Refrain from telling them to relax, have hope, that it will happen, etc.
- Ignore the urge to offer advice. Ask about their experience and what their doctor says about recommended treatment. Don't be offended if they don't share.

Instead of telling them to relax, invite them to do something that *is* relaxing!

Did I mention, please don't tell them to relax or to have fun trying?

Your loved ones won't tell you but hearing you say "relax" or "have fun trying" feels insensitive, irritating, and hurtful.

Cairn Community

During the last decade I developed a love of hiking and spending time in the great outdoors. In the process, I learned about stone formations called cairns.

Cairns are constructed to ensure the safety of hikers by showing the direction of paths, pointing to landmarks, and alerting to dangers on the trail. Often people will build their own cairns of remembrance for loved ones or their own personal stone formations to mark a successful hike to the top of a mountain.

I really like the idea of our being a cairn community and adding a stone of support to our loved ones' lives as they travel through their range of life with infertility. We can encourage and support as they climb out of the valley or weeds and travel up the peak of promise. By learning practical compassion we support the beautiful lives of the living.

Those traveling through infertility and childlessness first seek community with those who know their reality, usually through friends on the same path. While everyone has similarities, eventually each person finds resolution in different ways. The ones still uncertain of their fertility outcome usually feel left behind and alone.

Mary Lemonwater bares these emotions in a blog post: "One by one, my friends with infertility are becoming parents. Most have been so silent about their struggles that no one will know what they've been through. No one will know how strong they've had to be. Infertility affects one in eight couples. That is quite a lot, yet many of us feel like we're going through it alone."[38]

Infertility produces not only the aloneness of pain, but also the drifting that occurs when fellow infertiles become parents through a variety of means, and one person is left, facing a lonely reality. Western culture influences people to exist as silos, individually putting on brave faces and solving troubles with a solo mentality.

Hubbard shares more on the alone theme: "We adopt as a life script the myth of the rugged individual played out in Western movies where the cowboy hero rides off alone into the sunset."[39] She gives a community message of truth: "God declared Adam's aloneness not good; we are part of the whole body of Christ."[40]

People in the throes of raw pain and grief may knowingly or unknowingly choose isolation. The circle of community offers safe space to grieve and gain courage.

Family and Friends

Family and friends can provide a close sense of community for women in the midst of infertility and involuntary childlessness. These relationships can be either detrimental or supportive.

A few of the interviewees had negative experiences with friends who could not or would not support them during this time of need. However, Emily shared a positive friend development. She and her husband met a younger couple in Bible study and became close friends because of similar circumstances.

As a result, Emily and her husband became involved in the young family's life, spending holidays and vacations with the couple and their children. Their lives intertwined in a healthy, intergenerational manner, making the older couple feel they were truly part of a family.

Francine expressed thankfulness for the friends who showed her tenderness during her time after a late miscarriage and infant loss. She said, "They gave us an open space to cry. They were there."

Missy explained the need to talk about one's pain and experience: "Unless you talk about it, people won't ask. People don't tell you about their pregnancies because they think it will hurt your feelings. I'm the last one to know, but I'm really happy for others."

Lois's friend showed up with a big hug. In Lois's words, she "didn't say anything but 'I'm sorry.'"

Julia offered advice for practical action that family and friends can take to help: "Don't say 'call me.' Show up with dinner, offer to clean the house, mow the yard, or run errands. Leave a note on the door if it is not a good time to visit."

Jennifer told the story of her husband and his helpful reaction after one of her miscarriages. In an attempt to comfort her, he sat beside her and asked, "What do you need? Who do you need me to be?"

She described her relief knowing she could honestly share with him. Her mother also offered a beautiful gift of words when she validated Jennifer's pregnancy and lost child by describing the instant love affair that begins when pregnancy is confirmed.

Family and friend support makes a positive impact during and after the active infertility season. But it can also be negative.

The time of medical testing, procedures, and miscarriages can be a time of isolation and emotional pain. Two women sought discussion with friends when they were in the throes of their active infertility, and both were "shut down" and told they were not welcome to discuss their infertility. This caused them to withdraw from sharing with others and not speaking of their infertility challenges for years—in fact, until their interviews with me for this project.

A work colleague of Beth's said, "You're really nice. I thought you'd be selfish." Her co-worker said she made the assumption because Beth had no children.

Some also grew up in or married into cultures that held a high expectation of family and childbearing. The constant questions from family members about when they would have children became almost unbearable. The interactions finally resulted in some uncomfortable conversations about infertility and expectations.

Watching friends and family on social media has become a source of pain for these women as well, evoking a general feeling of inadequacy. The pictures flood their feeds: babies, family vacations, back to school, holidays, grandparent announcements . . . these are all pain triggers.

As mentioned, Elizabeth shared that the season of mourning for not being a grandparent has been worse than her original season of active infertility. She said her friends who were grandmothers focused mainly on activities with and conversations about their children and grandchildren. Elizabeth chose to spend time with younger women through activities such as mentoring and Bible studies.

These less-than-helpful examples of interpersonal interactions led the women to seek value in family and friend relationships. Several women experienced the joy and satisfaction of pouring into the lives of their nieces, nephews, godchildren, and friends' children.

The key for success in these situations was the willingness of siblings and friends to allow room for interaction and involvement.

Beth derived great meaning with her nieces and nephews until close involvement was no longer encouraged and, in fact, "busyness" got in the way. She felt as if her sister-in-law became protective of her own time and was unwilling to share her children with their aunt. Beth shared that she never tried to spend too much time or take over; she just loved her family. As a result of the rejection, Beth turned to her students and began to pour into their lives.

Helping Others

The childless woman may find life meaning and fruitfulness through mentoring and other areas of influence, both inside and outside of the church community.

When a woman is unable to give birth and has no children in her home, the root desire to make a difference often moves her to make sure her life has meaning and an impact for good.

Interviewees described the importance of people and support systems that propelled them to take meaningful steps in their journey. These women discovered opportunities to live out purpose and meaning through their communities of friends and neighbors.

Their stories and experiences prove that every individual's timeframe differs. Knowledge of this dynamic is key for the church and community to better understand ways to lovingly support those moving through their grief to find acceptance and new resolve.

During times of great trial, people tend toward self-focus. Yet problems loom larger, and the future looks bleaker in isolation.

When people step out of their pain to lend a hand to someone else, their horizon is broadened, their minds and bodies are given to the task of assistance, and the mental cycle of self-focus is broken. Often the other person's need is greater, and while the original pain is not removed, a new awareness of greater pain and need begins to form. Those who give and expect to help others often find that they themselves are blessed and helped far more than the help they offer.

Threads of this receive-by-giving reality were woven throughout the women's stories.

Elizabeth reached out to mentor younger women and counsel young seminary wives. As a couple, she and her husband reached into the lives of students through activities like potluck suppers.

Lois saw a great need and sought to serve on overseas mission trips.

René and her husband committed to babysitting and caring for other people's children.

Emily's sales revenue directly benefitted the family who adopted them as additional parents/grandparents.

Jennifer reached out through prison ministry to thousands of kids who needed guidance and the love of Jesus.

Julia said, "I can be an open book and talk to people. I'm open to talking to others about their pain."

**Everyone at the church and community table
needs love and grace.**

Women who walk through infertility into childlessness desired care and inclusion in the larger church family and in individual families. They search for meaning in their identity and fulfillment of God's purpose through the use of their talents and gifts to their community.

They also seek to help others in need. Doing so requires outreach from both sides. Those in the church and family communities must reach out to the involuntarily childless to include them.

What They Wish You Knew

The women who experience infertility and live in the light of their non-mom reality were asked to share nuggets of what they wished others knew about their overall experience and life. They offered general ideas as well as specifics:

Beth encouraged others not to make assumptions about anyone's life, especially those who tell you they do not have children. Be careful with probing questions when meeting someone socially if they do not fit a cultural standard.

Emily added another key ingredient to this line of questioning: "I wish people wouldn't assume that you didn't try hard enough."

Francine answered, "If you haven't been through it, it's so hard; it's a daily struggle and it doesn't go away. There's no timetable."

Missy wanted others to know how hard infertility treatment is on women's bodies. She said, "It is emotional and mental, but hard on the body, too, and feels unnatural to do all these things. Movies and TV make infertility look easy."

Your friend, relative, neighbor, or co-worker greatly appreciates your willingness to learn about her experience.

 Counter the twenty-eight-day cycle of fear with a calendar of love. Print a blank calendar for a specific month. Each day write an inspirational quote, Scripture, funny saying, or simply, "I'm praying for you" or "Thinking of you today." Give the calendar to your friend with a note of support.

Chapter 5
Sacred Support

I lay on my sofa in a fog of misery. Curled up in a ball to protect my stomach pain, I pondered what in the world to do now.

My third and final pregnancy was declared over, and the conclusion included a surgical procedure. My sweats and tee shirt were wrinkled, my hair was a mess, and any makeup once applied had been swept away by the torrent of tears. Residual effects of anesthesia began to pass as I lay in silence.

The doorbell rang, and I unwisely made my way to answer. Hunched over in pain, I unlocked and opened the door. There stood a sweet couple from my neighborhood. They were older and I knew them as caring, devout Christians.

As soon as the door opened, they swept in, came into the living room, and sat down on my sofa, patting a space for me in between them. The wife knew of my situation because I had told her the sad outcome when she called the day before to check on my pregnancy status. They took no notice of my unkempt state as they moved my blanket and pillow to the floor to create space to sit down.

They had one goal and one goal only: to share the Word of God in order to comfort me in my time of need.

As I sat (stunned and silent) between them, they each opened their Bibles and began reciting Scripture. They took turns reading aloud life-giving words and explaining how much God loved me and how he works through life pain, in tough times, etc.

I don't recall too much of what they specifically said over the next forty-five minutes.

Here is what I do remember:

> I remember feeling ambushed—by their words and their actions.

> I remember feeling a silent scream deep within but could not summon the courage or words to tell them I needed them to leave.

> I remember feeling a huge anger well up at God. The more of his Word they shared, the angrier I felt at his inaction in my life.

I guess they sought to "comfort" and "help" but all they did was stir up resentment towards God and towards their ignorance of my situation and what seemed to be calloused behavior.

They didn't ask me to communicate anything, they just recited a lot of Christianese that seemed rehearsed for any occasion, regardless of the need to ask what was individually, personally needed in a specific situation.

They didn't share their heart or ask about mine. They just spoke words that fell dead on my ears.

When, finally, they ran out of words and left, I curled up with my dog and sobbed until I fell asleep.

I share this story to help fellow believers understand that there is a time and place to share God's truth and his Word with people in raw pain. We are called to love one another, and one of the most loving acts you can do is sit in the awkward place of pain and just *be* with the other person.

God's Word is beauty, life, and love and there is an appropriate time to share and study this together. The newness of pain and grief may not be the right time.

Please seek God's guidance when you know there is new loss. Gain permission to sit in that sacred pain space. This is about them, not you. You must be willing to give them what they need, not what makes you comfortable.

True family community in the church requires a dance of reaching in to someone else's pain and those in pain reaching out to grasp the "hand of God" offered through family care.

Your willingness to help your brothers and sisters in the church family illustrates Christ's love in action.

Social Media Impact

The influential culture of social media has grown dramatically in recent years. Infertility that once isolated many women presents an "in your face" opportunity to purge pain through technology.

Social media provides an environment for expression that can be both negative and positive. For example, one social-media platform reveals an abundance of infertility wounds and an outpouring of frustration and pain. One person posted a photo of a negative pregnancy test with a middle finger salute super imposed on top.

Social media allows the outpouring of grief and the baring of souls. People voice pain, but what fills them with hope and moves them onward?

Equipping the church to reach out to couples in need with understanding, compassion, and love is essential to living out the Great Commission and the Greatest Commandments—both on the part of patients and those who minister to them.[41]

Social media allows anyone and everyone to have a voice. The anonymity of a computer screen offers the opportunity to hurl words with little thought to their impact. Most people, including those in the church, need to redirect words and actions that inflict pain to words and actions that promote healing and love.

One Facebook post by Stacy Halstead presented an honest description of pregnancy trials. At the end of her post, she thanked everyone for reading and allowing her to share. She did not ask for advice, help, stories, or criticism, but she received all of these in droves. Throughout the hundred comments reviewed (out of thousands), there were countless episodes of thoughtless comments, many from Christians.[42]

This example reflects the need for a compassionate sharing of encouragement and hope to persons experiencing loss.

Not long ago I heard from a friend about a blog post detailing another's struggle to have a child. The woman poured her heart out and detailed where they were as a couple and how she was processing their situation. She had a toddler and they were having difficulty with secondary infertility (infertility experienced after successful pregnancy and birth).

My friend was outraged at the response and comments under the blog post. Lots of advice, wisdom, and sharing *better left unwritten.*

Here are a few paraphrased samples:

You should never give up; God will give you another child.

You have a child and need to be content.

Where is your trust? There is a plan and you need to trust more and be faithful.

You get the idea. I really believe for the most part people just don't know what to say and they don't like to hover in that awkward place.

I understand.

It would be supportive to say something positive:

> Proud of you and will pray for you in your continued journey.

> Thank you for sharing your heart. Holding your family close in thought and prayer.

> Appreciate your courage in sharing your story.

When we read social media stories and posts, let's say something brief and positive or write nothing at all.

When we are face-to-face with loved ones, let's sit with them in the discomfort and choose to let it be okay, following their lead to be silent support or a listening ear.

Remember, infertility strikes at the very essence of who we are as human beings. And for those with a biblical worldview, this goes right back to Genesis, the creation of man and woman, and God's mandate to be fruitful and multiply.

Generational Inclusion

The two generations with the largest populations are key to include in the church family: Millennials, who are predicted to delay having children and therefore increase the likelihood for infertility and childlessness, and Baby Boomers with no children in the home.

It is up to the local church to determine how to engage these populations in meaningful and intergenerational ways.

Current data shows Millennials postponing marriage and childbirth for several reasons, one of them being financial. Susan Heavey, writing for *Health Journalism*, explores the resulting delay:

> Many questions remain about family formation in the post recession (sic) economy," researchers at the Urban Institute wrote in a recent paper, noting that answers won't come until that generation "has completed its reproductive years." And while some Americans have increasingly put off having children until their later years, the possibility of an entire generation delaying parenthood is forcing a reexamination of the social impact of fertility.[43]

In a 2015 report, *Infertility in America*, conducted by Reproductive Medicine Associates of New Jersey, a quote from the findings is as follows: "In general, our report found that many misconceptions remain about infertility procedures that can impact patient outcomes."[44]

The Reproductive Medicine Association report also references the CDC report about declining birthrates in the US. It states, "Furthermore, our own proprietary survey found that Millennials aren't planning to start having children until their early to mid-30s, which could drive infertility rates even higher and birth rates even lower."[45]

In an interview with Erika Janes for *Parents Magazine*, Dr. Shefali Shastri, M.D., with Reproductive Medical Associates of New Jersey, elaborates on the misconceptions of age and fertility.

Shastri shares a three-fold reason, starting with the idea that "Thirty is the new twenty." "'While this may hold true in other aspects of life and health, this doesn't apply to human reproduction,' she says. 'Despite education, it may be difficult to accept the concept that we can't stop the clock.' Additionally, we read about older couples having babies and don't always hear the full details (donor eggs, surrogacy, etc)."[46]

Women who are involuntarily childless are not the only ones without children who need to be considered in church demographics. Elinor Burkett expounds on the choices made by the large generation of Baby Boomers. She writes, "Baby-boomer women—the first women in world history to grow up with the ability to have sex without reproductive consequences—have opted out of motherhood in record numbers. Choosing careers over family, committed to population control, or simply not interested in kids, one-fifth of them are childless by choice."[47]

Church members include women who were unable to conceive, women who chose not to conceive, women who adopted, and women who are considered empty nesters—their children are grown and out of the house.

All of these women are members of the church family, serve an important role in life and ministry, and have value to contribute. Those who are involuntarily childless have a particular need to uncover meaningful connections and contributions in their lives.

A research report published in Europe's *Journal of Psychology* by Sumaira Malik and Neil Coulson details a study conducted to determine the role an online support community played in the lives of women who were involuntarily, permanently childless. One of the central themes found in the postings related to coming to terms with childlessness and the researchers provided the following in their study results:

> In addition, some women spoke of the need to "reinvent" themselves through seeking out new activities and social groups as well as finding a new sense of purpose and meaning to their life. This appeared to be a central part of the process of coming to terms with childlessness and

accessing the online support community was often viewed as a first step in this process.[48]

This illustrates the importance of women finding a meaning and purpose outside of themselves to move in a positive direction in their lives rather than getting stuck in the mire of disappointment and non-motherhood.

No matter the reason, those in the church who are childless desire a place in the church family culture.

The spiritual impact differs for those who desired a family although *all* childless persons in the body of Christ are part of God's family and have a place within the church community.

Spiritual Impact

In *Reconceiving Infertility*, Candida Moss and Joel Baden explore biblical narratives of barren women. They write:

> The default state of humanity is not fertile. God must "open the womb." And, as the stories of the matriarchs make clear, even in cases of morally perfect women, sometimes God neglects this sacred and promised duty. It is natural to want to attribute blame. But the matriarchal narratives, and the Near Eastern cultural context in which they participate, ensure that the blame does not lie with the infertile woman.[49]

Reconceiving Infertility provides clarity for the often-misunderstood application of the barren stories found in the Bible.

Components of a Fruitful Life

The Christian walk becomes more intentional when one knows his or her gifts, purpose, and identity. Every Christian possesses the foundational purpose to love God, love others, proclaim Jesus, and know their true identity as a child of the King. This is imperative for the assurance of the human role in the overarching story of God's redemption. Scripture illustrates the truth that child production is not the only path to a godly, fruitful life in Jesus. Many people, including Christians, place the notion of success or failure in life on their ability to have children.

Moss and Baden provide additional interpretation of a sense of fruitfulness that can result: "The Bible abounds with childless, even unmarried, perfectly natural and judgment-free individuals. The raising of 'be fruitful and multiply' to a universal and timeless divine imperative is an interpretive choice. It is not demanded by the text; in fact it ignores important aspects of the text's presentation of this blessing."[50]

Ultimately, those in the church family enrich their ministry to fellow believers with such a biblical understanding about fruitfulness; however, great care must be taken with those they want to impress with this truth due to the painful loss of the mom dream.

Hubbard emphasizes the message of life by God's transformation:

> God means for us through His grace to redeem our pain—to use it as a journey into joy and maturity. He means for us to be more than survivors; He means for us to be conquerors in every circumstance of life, however difficult that circumstance may be. . . No matter how terrible the events through which we must live, it is God's intention for us to be transformed, not destroyed. Now that is good news.[51]

Guiding with grace and honest family care assists others in seeking God and his direction to stay the course in life and identity.

Author Judith Stigger depicts the thought process within the person who grapples with life within the reality of infertility: "When the infertile person says, 'I have put myself through enough pain; if I am infertile, so be it,' the person's attention shifts from 'Why am I infertile?' to 'How am I going to live with being infertile?'"[52]

A testimony of God's greatness develops when the individual seeks the answer in this seismic shift.

Identity

One way to experience the transformation to living with infertility is a renewed understanding of identity. Labels obtained and responsibilities performed are not a person's identity. They are descriptives of life positions and activities. A Christian's root identity is found in knowing and belonging to the Lord.

Hubbard offers a fresh perspective about pain's influence on circumstances: "Pain pushes us to rethink and redefine the basic beliefs about worth and value that form the infrastructure of our lives. At this point we may find that we have unwittingly absorbed the cultural belief that how I look and what I do equal who I am."[53]

When identity is in question, the tendency to ask *why* looms as well, and Patricia Taylor expresses the influence over true identity and value:

> *Why* keeps me from being who God created me to be, because I am constantly afraid that none of it was real. I keep waiting for the other shoe to drop, because I am afraid I really am not worthy. I continue to hold on to the lies I have been told and believed all my life—that I am worthless and will never amount to anything. I keep believing that my life will always be a shambles and that any time of joy will be short-lived and fruitless. But, these are all lies designed by the enemy

of my soul to keep me from being effective—to keep me from becoming the woman God created me to be.[54]

Women are first and foremost to love and serve God. Messages from the Christian subculture must communicate this truth clearly without a motherhood expectation that adds pressure and heartache.

Gifts

Those who seek meaning in their lives, who want to experience fruitful purpose, succeed by using their talents and gifts. In her book about infertility, Melissa Ford advises making decisions within infertility from an understanding of one's identity and abilities: "Own your foibles and your strengths, and use them to live here well. In other words, always be yourself, even within infertility."[55]

More specifically, to live life using one's gifts is to honor and love God and to serve his people. As Mowczko explains,

> Parenthood may well be the main ministry of some men and women, and this needs to be encouraged. However, many men and women also have other expressions of their calling as Jesus' disciples. They have been given other ministry gifts, roles, and functions to use outside of their immediate or

extended families. These other ministries should also be encouraged.[56]

Offering classes and workshops on spiritual gifts enables all church members to learn where God might use them to serve one another—information that will help not only those in the midst of infertility, but also church members in general.

Glahn and Cutrer offer a poignant view and ask a raw question with regard to the gift of children: "The Bible says, 'Children are a gift from the Lord; the fruit of the womb is His reward' (Ps. 127:3). Does that mean I don't qualify?"[57] The authors describe the ultimate gift of salvation that is enough for all. Then they offer, "God blesses all of His children, but He chooses to distribute specific gifts differently. These gifts are not limited to children, nor are babies His 'ultimate' gift."[58]

When encouraging others to use their gifts and talents in the midst of loss and reality, the would-be encourager must take care with regard to time and place.

Stigger emphasizes the responsibility of Christian action in patience and assurance:

> Finally, the Christian is called to encourage and challenge the infertile person to relate to and serve others, but not to judge if the infertile person does not immediately respond to this call. The infertile person's energy is depleted, and a pause for rest and reorientation is needed.

Even Jesus went off by himself for a 40-day retreat to consider his own identity and role as the Son of God, before beginning his ministry to others (Matt. 4:1–11).[59]

Patience, love, presence, and grace extended by friends and loved ones help the infertile person to move further towards a fruitful life despite the loss of their dream.

Church Family

Many evangelical churches treat Sunday as a biological family day to the exclusion of the spiritual family. Consequently, Sunday can be the loneliest day of the week for those without children. To shift the biological-family focus to a spiritual-family focus, churches might ask couples without children to serve in areas normally reserved for parents of children (mission trips, musical events, fundraisers).

These couples may find meaning for themselves and contribute to healthy congregations, enable general wellbeing and development of the next generation, assist parents, strengthen communities, and undergird the church family.

The church family can communicate awareness of involuntary childlessness by educating from the pulpit and holding workshops and sponsoring speakers. They can create space corporately and individually in the church body and model the family table.

A post by Barry Jones, seminary professor and senior pastor, describes the biblical and relational importance of what he calls "Table Fellowship": "Tables are one of the most important places of human connection. We're often most fully alive to life when sharing a meal around a table. We shouldn't be surprised, then, to find that throughout the Bible God has a way of showing up at tables."[60]

Intentional interaction and life investment in the lives of members without children will broaden areas of ministry, enhance the body of Christ, and promote fruitful opportunities within the church and greater community.

The church community has a God-ordained responsibility to love their neighbor with compassion and outreach. Those who come to a new place of knowledge, acceptance, and understanding of God's sovereign hand must also reach out to their church community and look for ways to be involved and love their neighbor as well.

What the Church Can Do

- Be aware. The church must learn about the painful experiences of infertility and involuntary childlessness.

- Be intentionally inviting. The outreach of loving members of God's family should include intentional invitations to serve and participate.

- Be the hands and feet of Christ. René encouraged those in community to "care for people, not cure them—not necessarily with words." Invoke acts of kindness and care to show Jesus's love to brothers and sisters. During the active infertility season, provide a meal, schedule a time to go sit and read or watch a movie with them, invite them to an art museum, show, or other non-child-related event, or take them on a nature walk. When the woman has a surgical procedure, show up and quietly sit in the waiting room with her spouse. Be present.

- Ask them to serve in their giftedness. Caution: be careful about recruiting them to work in the nursery or in any "glorified babysitter opportunities."

- Show interest, not judgment. Proceed with great care before offering any opinion (or "biblical truth") about infertility treatment, adoption, or any other personal choices.

- Listen. Do not probe. Offer to hear their stories, pain, and hope. Exercise thoughtful care with delicate questions. These women need to be heard and not questioned unnecessarily.

- Invite and clearly offer grace. The women interviewed wanted to be included in news about families and events. Keep expectations of infertility patients' involvement to a minimum. There is an individual fine line for each situation. They want an invitation to the baby shower or toddler birthday along with the freedom to politely decline.

- Include. Do not ignore. Create non-mom space and activities for the childless women in your church to participate in discipleship and growth. Build additional opportunities that are not mom- or family-focused.

- Offer relationship, not advice. Walk with the childless women in companionship without giving opinions, sharing "success" stories, or offering third-party medical tips. These women spend enough time desperately searching for answers and are well aware of opportunities and treatments. Success stories offer only false hope or add to feelings of failure.

What Individuals in Community Can Do

- Galvanize churches to action with those who are childless in their midst.

- Coordinate a gathering of women who are childless—for meet-ups or online live discussions to help them support one another.

- Develop retreat workshops for Mother's Day weekends.

- Offer resources, volunteer positions, and brainstorm opportunities within the community on how to be involved and make a difference. Give these women a voice and a place to mentor if they so desire.

- For those women in the early days of their childlessness adjustment—help them know they are not alone and give older childless women a place to have their stories told and influence others for good. Include them in your family events, invite them to children's musical programs, concerts, or game night and dinner in your home. Remember to also offer grace and understanding if they decline participation.

Jennifer summed up the heart of this desire to live a life of meaning: "God never wastes anything in our lives; He uses *everything* to bless, grow, teach, confirm, encourage, and sanctify us. If sharing my journey can help someone—anyone—even in a small way, it means my pain had a purpose, and my babies are helping others even though they never drew breath on this earth."

For those in the church and community seeking ways to minister and reach out, these women offer a glimpse of their holiday pain. Margot explained that every holiday potentially holds pain—Halloween, Thanksgiving, and Christmas. Beth would not go to church and hear sermons about mothers on Mother's Day.

As individuals, and as a church community, we can offer understanding and support for the women and men in our midst who are childless and hurting. Beth's friend came up to her after a baby shower and said, "I bet today was really hard for you."

Francine told of a friend who convinced her to join a prayer group. "I realized that everybody needs help. We can help each other through God's Word. Her invitation got me out of the house and into this group, and also to an infertility workshop."

Missy received a phone call from a female leader in the church to pray about her role in a leadership opportunity.

Not only can the community reach out, but those who are hurting can also move through their pain and love their neighbors. René learned to pay attention to the needs in the church: "There are always needs in community. I had to look past my pain and realize I am a vessel. God, how are you going to use me? By using me, you fill me up."

Elizabeth encouraged others to use creative thinking and resolutions: "Be willing to be available and intentionally involved." Beth did not go to baby showers but she sent handcrafted baby gifts. Emily prayed for pregnant parents to love their children and raise them in a Christian home.

Lois described her baby shower attendance: "If I'm close to them, I'll go to a baby shower now. I do want to celebrate with them. I don't want *their* baby; I want *my* baby."

M. Gay Hubbard elaborates on the importance of life understanding:

Stripped to its basic elements, choosing life is a decision we make—and make again—to undertake responsible self-care that enables us to survive and thrive in ways that glorify God. As Christians, we believe that acceptance of God's gift of life in Christ is foundational to self-care. But in the context of this basic step, we understand that we must also work out self-care in the specifics of faith-based living when life becomes messy and complex.[61]

Encouragement toward self-care requires a careful, non-threatening establishment of trust between persons reaching out to those in infertility and those in the midst of infertility and loss. The timeline of grief is different for everyone. Difficulties arise when the hurting soul meets impatience and a lack of compassion in people offering their help.

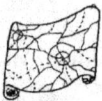

Write down five of your favorite Bible verses about joy and thankfulness and email them to your friend in the midst of infertility.

Church

Local churches often create a sense of "family culture" in which the emphasis falls on the nuclear or biological family. Rachel Giles chronicles one woman's experience:

Mrs. Lowrie has found going to church hard during her struggle with childlessness. "It feels as though the family unit is something that is celebrated a lot, and it makes you feel as though you're lacking in some way. I found secular environments so much easier to be in. At work, I felt quite normal: a lot of people get married later, and don't have children. Work was often like a retreat; church was stressful."[62]

Infertile couples and those without children must be included in the local church community. Research on grief, coping with loss, and reaching out to others shows the effect on the life of a woman without children. In *More Than an Aspirin*, Hubbard discusses redemptive management and stewardship of pain as follows:

A redemptive stewardship of pain does not depend upon the answer to the "why" question that we may ultimately work out. Our part in bringing about a good outcome is not simply a matter of thinking differently *about* pain, although that too happens on the journey. Redemptive stewardship is faith-based living—head *and* heart— into and through the pain. It is living the questions in such a way that we live our way into a new relationship with God and with ourselves. It is living into a new kinship and community with each other and into a new understanding of the world and the journey by which we have come into a new place.[63]

God created humans to live in community and communicates through himself and through Scripture a message of unity and love. He calls upon the church to pass down faith *to* and *through* children and families. The Holy Spirit creates a family within the church. Understanding on a scale beyond the nuclear family is imperative for people without children and for members of the Body of Christ.

One way to assist is through a loving approach and truthful communication about the family "promises" of children. Glahn and Cutrer provide a concrete example of the biblical promise:

> If Christians take the promise given to Sarah and claim that the same promise has been given to us, we're distorting what the text says. A promise made in the Bible to an individual is not a promise made to everybody for always. If your parents promised you a bike for Christmas, that promise applies to you and only you, not to your neighbor five generations from now.[64]

A truthful directive needs to be gently shared when a family member wonders why God has not fulfilled the "promise of a child" in his or her life.

Church community can emphasize the call to be fruitful in the midst of God's family, not in the fulfillment of a biological family. This is a message used to kindly encourage one who feels useless in the midst of barrenness. Moss and Baden examine the foundation of the biblical family:

While Mark [the Gospel writer] never discusses infertility, his portrait of the Holy Family is of interest to us precisely because it is not predicated on biology. As we tease out the significance of the baptism and Jesus's divine sonship, we shall see a model of parenting accessible to everyone and, crucially, divorced from individual procreation and procreative abilities. [65]

Every person in the universal church is part of God's family and actions toward one another should enhance inclusion and involvement.

Beverly Hislop underscores the challenge that those in the midst of grief face. She writes, "Unfortunately, many women have stated that the church has not been a 'safe' place for them. Often their faith is challenged by having prayers unanswered; and songs of praise are hard to sing when their hearts are hurting. It is hard to grieve publicly when the source of the sorrow is so private." [66]

Believers are called to love one another, and that involves the action of reaching into another's life with support. Winter provides guidance in the ways of stepping into the grief of others:

In Western culture, people who are grieving often feel very isolated, and because they don't know what to say or do, well-meaning neighbors and friends tend to avoid or try not to upset the one who is grieving. They are often more uncomfortable with the pain than is the one who is grieving. But it is important to try to seek good friends and to be a good friend.[67]

The church family must "mourn with those who mourn." Practical action is a presence provided in the midst of uncomfortable uncertainty, showing up to offer care and community in a time of need.

One of the most difficult days in the life of the church is Mother's Day. The annual reminder of what is not to be keeps many women from worship on that day.

To realize the far-reaching tentacles, observe what occurs in the culture as described by Ellen Walker: "According to the National Retail Foundation, Mother's Day is a 14-billion-dollar industry. According to Mother's Day Central, restaurants in the United States claim that it's their busiest day of the entire year!"[68]

Understanding, inclusion, and acknowledgment in church gatherings on Mother's Day go a long way to offer a balm to a woman's seared soul.

Terri Stovall describes the grace and purpose found when women exercise mothering in the church:

> There are many girls and young women in this world who need spiritual mothering and long to have an older woman who loves, teaches, nurtures, corrects and protects them. God's grace propels us to nurture,

mother and invest in the lives of young women and, often, it is when we answer this command that we run headlong into God's grace and our grief is replaced by purpose.[69]

The opportunity to act in mothering ways transforms numbness and grief into thriving life. People live out their purpose using their God-given talents and gifts. In addition to finding one's purpose and using one's gifts to glorify God, the believer also ministers out of his or her pain.

Doing so raises a question about members facing infertility and/or a future of involuntary childlessness: What does the church do for those in pain? And what do those in pain do to cope with the loss of their dream?

Many churches have no mechanism in place for discussing and intentionally investing in the lives of members and reaching out in love into the community. Hislop makes the following observation related to helping infertile couples in the church:

> Although some churches have support groups for those dealing with infertility, many women have not found this type of resource available. Starting a group for people to share their hurts and hopes with others who have the same concerns and emotions would be a wonderful resource. One woman stated she had attended a secular support group but did not feel like she could connect or identify with the women there

because the comfort and healing of the heavenly Comforter was not a part of the process.[70]

Groups or ministries reaching out from the church to her members and surrounding community extend the love of God by helping women in the midst of infertility and those reeling from the realization that their dreams of motherhood will not come to fruition.

Marni Rosner urges leaders to consider the care of their congregants:

> In addition, there is clearly a need for further training in theological education. Considering the emphasis on procreation in religion, and the sudden loss of connection many experienced in their places of worship, religious leaders require further education regarding the psychological and psychosocial consequences of infertility. Churches, temples, and other places of worship have the potential to be tremendous sources of comfort for those struggling with this issue.[71]

It is imperative that spiritual leaders grow in biblical and life discernment in the realm of infertility and childlessness.

Biblical Call

Christians are called to love God, love one another, and make disciples. Personal identity is rooted in Jesus; unique gifts and talents are endowed to each; and a community of fellow believers and church family surround in support. Jesus said he came to serve and not to be served (Mark 10:45). Believers are to do the same, regardless of hindrance or perceived default, and Stigger clearly calls all to fulfill their role in God's plan:

> God answers each limitation and then orders, "Now, go! I will help you . . ." (Exod. 4:12 TEV). Since my infertility does not rob me of the capacity to minister to my neighbor, it does not excuse me from my obligation to act in God's service to my neighbor.[72]

God calls and equips believers, but most importantly, they have the presence of God empowering them to fulfill his call to love and action.

The call to love includes those that are infertile, and the content of that love includes telling the truth about how God has created each person. Glahn and Cutrer hone in on the soul-deep truth of earthly life as a follower of Jesus Christ: "We have no promise that he will give us any temporal benefits. And even if God does answer the prayer for children, those blessings will never satisfy us at the deepest levels of our souls. Only intimacy with the Father through the Son satisfies the soul's deepest longings."[73]

The truthful foundation of Christian faith resonates within and serves as a loving reminder for persons in the midst of infertility (in a timely, caring manner).

Practical Service

What responsive actions can church family members extend to help their brothers and sisters during and after a season of infertility and possibly into the real world of childlessness?

Hubbard offers a practical principle to enact life-changing care for fellow human beings:

> One of the most important things we need is people who can be present with us, who can simply be with us in our pain, those who can be fully aware of the intensity of our grief and loss yet feel unafraid, those who can come into our chaos and disorientation without becoming in turn disoriented by it. We need people who can see with the eyes of their hearts, so to speak, and understand that to be present is to lessen the aloneness and help us hold a space where hope can come. Those who bring the gift of presence have an inner matter-of-fact calmness and patience in the face of pain that permits them to come and "sit a bit" until things "settle out," as a country neighbor once said to me.[74]

Showing care with presence is a comforting practice. Silence helps, and so do words of comfort. Such words can include simple phrases like, "I care about you," "I am so sorry for your loss," and "I am praying for your comfort and peace." Often out of the speaker's discomfort, words are spoken that contribute more pain than peace.

When a miscarriage, or stillbirth occurs, there is a loss of *life*. One must acknowledge this. Talk about it.

If there is unexplained infertility and inability to get pregnant, there is the loss of a dream. Acknowledge this. Talk about it.

Pat answers, clichés, and solution statements do not provide comfort.

Relating to words of comfort, Jill Bialosky and Helen Schulman share stories from a variety of writers. They summarize:

> Somehow the messages that we received regarding our miscarriages and pregnancy losses were that this child wasn't meant to be, and in that message was also the fallacy that they weren't to be mourned. And when something can't be mourned, talked about, allowed to be real, the experience becomes ensconced in a cloud of shame.[75]

Learning to be comfortable with discomfort while sitting and "mourning with those who mourn" will transform relationships and grow community.

Resources in the Church

Church activities and publications provide some memorial space for persons experiencing loss. Pregnancy and Infant Loss Awareness (PILA) Lubbock, Texas, holds an annual memorial service in a local church.

In an article written by Dennise Krause and published by the Orthodox Church, the writer says,

> Fr. John Breck writes of the mother who has miscarried, "Her pain needs to be acknowledged, accepted, and palliated through words and gestures of understanding, sympathy and love, offered by her family and the parish community." In reality, most of the parents who experience the loss of a child during pregnancy, suffer alone. This is especially true in the instance of early pregnancy loss (i.e. miscarriages and ectopic pregnancies) where there is no "body" to be seen and often the mother shows no outward signs of pregnancy.[76]

The site also offers medical understanding, counseling and prayer services.

A variety of church support groups exist for infertility and miscarriage as well as numerous published works and online groups with devotional and support information.

The importance of healthy grief cannot be overstated, and the above resources and church memorial services hold up a healing, affirming example of true family support and recognition of those who have lost children and pregnancies.

In *Empty Arms*, Pam Vredevelt describes her pastor's words to the congregation upon the return of her husband and herself after loss:

> Many of you know that John and Pam were expecting a baby. That baby is now with the Lord . . . Now listen to me and listen well . . . They don't need any "words from God" or "inspired exhortations" or advice. They just need you to love them and hug them and let them work through their grief. There will be a point where sympathy will no longer be needed or wanted, so please be sensitive to them and just allow them to be themselves.[77]

The pastor modeled a caring example of powerful words and wise counsel before the family community.

Resources in the Community

The annual National Pregnancy and Infant Loss Awareness Month in October creates a beautiful calendar space to promote understanding about this topic. Dawn Friedman shares insight in her post on the importance of personal grieving:

Although pregnancy loss is so common, living through it can leave us feeling isolated and alone. People don't acknowledge our grief or say the wrong thing ("Oh well, you can always try again") or we may feel that we don't have the right to be sad because the pregnancy was "so early" or because we had some ambivalence about it. You have a right to grieve no matter the context and timing of your pregnancy.[78]

Friedman's blog post also offers information for a Tulip Bulb Planting Ceremony held by a support group in remembrance of pregnancy loss.

In Honolulu, Hawaii, the Perinatal Bereavement Network organizes a service each year during which participants are invited to light a candle and place a poem or photograph in a communal scrapbook to honor and remember "a baby lost."

St. Francis Hospital in Hartford, Connecticut, offers interdenominational memorial services for mourning loss; a recent conference of the International Stillbirth Alliance offered activity stations for bereaved families to "create memories" through journaling, scrapbooking, and memory kits[79]; and the Winthrop-University Hospital (in Mineola, New York) Perinatal Bereavement Team sponsors a Walk to Remember each year. A Buddhist ritual mourns the unborn dead as well.[80]

Medical centers, faiths other than Christianity, and organizations reach out to enfold infertile couples/loss parents. How much more should the church, the Body of Christ, live out love with its family in the midst of what is one of the most stressful, heart-wrenching seasons of life?

Conclusion

Leaders and members of the church family fulfill a crucial role in aiding those in grief and loss, by living out God's love in a tangible way, beginning with the act of prayer. Hislop communicates this necessity: "Most importantly, be a prayer supporter. Pray for the childless in your church. 'Carry each other's burdens, and in this way you will fulfill the law of Christ' (Gal 6:2)."[81]

All who walk the road of infertility and childlessness need love, support, insight, and understanding. Stigger underscores the believer's Christ-like action in order to show Christ to the one in pain and doubt:

> It is the privilege of Christians to act as God's emissaries to infertile individuals. "So we are ambassadors for Christ, God making his appeal through us" (2 Cor 5:20). Because the infertile person experiences uncertainty about the nature, intent or even existence of God, the person is particularly sensitive to the kindness or callousness of Christians.[82]

Creating the community and environment conducive to a true

family, the family of God requires intentionality and effort on the part of her members. Brownback sums up the biblical family:

> "Her children rise up and call her blessed; her husband also, and he praises her" (Prov 31:28). In a loving family, the members recognize the value of each other. Here the children and the husband offer their praise. God places a high premium on family. The whole course of redemptive history is built on the family structure, which began when God instructed his people to be fruitful and multiply (Gen 1:28).[83]

The New Testament marks a shift from the extended biological family to the spiritual family. In the context of the gathered church, God intends each member of the family feel included in the big, eternal love of the church as she fulfills her divine calling.

Chapter 6
A Prescription for Doctors & Staff

***

To the doctors, nurses, and medical staff working with infertility patients, your sensitive and informed participation in this journey is critical to their well being.

***

Along the infertility road, "medical" advice comes in many forms and from many sources, including friends with experience in the fertility trenches.

When sperm testing time came around, the combination of advice proved helpful in the midst of the humiliation:

> *Make sure you screw the lid on tight and place the plastic cup in a brown paper lunch bag to transport it to the lab.*

> *Remember you only have an hour to get to the lab destination. You need to hurry and at the same time you must keep it warm.*

Be sure to hold the bag between your legs as your drive to maintain a good temperature for testing.

My doctor was just as specific:

Remember you must have the specimen to the lab by 9:00am.

The specimen is only good for one hour.

You must deliver it within that timeframe or we will need to start over.

I struggled with the thought of making the request for the sperm specimen. I mean, the entire infertility journey involves multiple opportunities to take on blame and/or inadequacy or contribute to your spouse feeling that way too.

All the other operational specifics piled on and left me completely stressed out. I was a mess and certainly didn't want to have a *Groundhog Day* movie re-living of this morning over and over again.

The fateful morning arrived and I took the plastic cup (lid secured) and gingerly placed it in the brown paper bag, got behind the wheel of my car, and put the bag between my knees. The lab was a forty-five-minute drive with traffic, and I was overwhelmed with urgency to deliver the package.

With a sigh of relief I parked the car, rode up the elevator, and opened the door to the lab.

The smiling face on the wall said 8:55. I exhaled every bit of humiliation and stress and went to the window to hand it over. There was no one in the waiting room and only one person behind the glass. She looked up, gave a vague smile, then glanced down at my brown paper bag.

Her smile turned upside down.

At this point I was holding the package away from me as if it were a ticking bomb. I just wanted to finish this task.

In two seconds her frown became an all out scowl and with a shake of her head she jerked open the window and asked what I needed.

I stammered and explained the obvious. She replied with disbelief.

> *They didn't get the memo. I can't believe they didn't get the memo.*

> *I'm sorry?*

> *The memo. I can't understand why people don't read their memos.*

Her finger pointed in disgust to the lifeline of matter surrendered for testing. I looked at the clock ticking away . . . 8:57.

Ma'am, please, just take this sample. My doctor's office sent me here and I must give this to you for testing right now. It has been almost an hour and as you know, I need to have this tested within an hour or the sample will no longer be viable.

I can't help you. We don't do those tests here anymore.

What?!

Have you heard about those out-of-body experiences where people swear they are floating above the room and can see their body and the medical personnel working on them? Yep, I know the feeling.

You have to drive it across town. (She named a city thirty minutes away.)

The memo said it all. We don't do that here. You must drive to the other lab.

As she shut the glass, I resorted to full-on begging.

Please take this bag. I'm out of time. There is no way I can make it to the other location. Is there nothing you can do to help me?

I can't help it if they didn't get the memo.

In life, I seek to offer kindness to strangers but by this point I think you might be able to guess the advice and action I wanted to suggest regarding the memo. She turned her back on me. My head hung low and I carried my brown bag of burden to the restroom down the hall. I couldn't believe this. I was one part defeated, one part angry, and one part small.

So. Very. Small.

I prayed a quick prayer, shrugged my shoulders, and tossed my precious package into the public restroom trashcan. I made it all the way to the car before I dissolved into tears.

Eventually we met success with the test. I made it to the correct lab in a timely fashion.

There are many stories and examples of pain and humiliation from people who share their infertility walk. The memo incident is but one that I personally experienced.

The tests that couples endure have many levels of humiliation. They are invasive, extensive, scary, sometimes painful, and always serve to enhance our insecurities both individually and as a couple.

Medical Encounters

Along with data about general Western culture characteristics, the women also shared their experiences with the medical community. These varied with each woman and reflected opposite ends of the spectrum. That is, some were quite negative while others were positive.

None of the women were neutral about their medical care. Unhelpful, even hurtful, experiences created feelings of disconnection and emotional chaos. Several women remembered little in terms of doctor engagement, reassurance, or an overall treatment plan.

Missy described her medical experience as impersonal fertility mills.

Francine's infant-loss trauma resulted in questions about her medical care. After much anger and heartache, she realized she "had to let go—could not live there in the anger."

Jennifer walked into her doctor's office and noticed her patient folder had a large red stamp that read, "Advanced Maternal Age." This was the first she heard of her medical category.

The medical community inadvertently added to the emotional pain of numerous women with discussions of egg quality. Aging eggs are a reality in the infertility process, but this detrimental label can subconsciously add to the layers of pain and stress on the female patients.

A particularly harmful term used in the medical community is the clinical term for miscarriage—referred to as "spontaneous abortion." Because the term "abortion" also describes when a female *chooses* to end a pregnancy, for women desperately seeking to get pregnant and give birth to her child, this term wreaks emotional havoc.

If medical personnel seek to offer genuine care, they need to become aware of the pain inflicted and change the labels applied to procedures and the women undergoing treatment.

Many of the women experienced quality care from their doctors, nurses, and staff. Several described their doctors as "compassionate and loving," "supportive," "offering sincere prayers," and "reassurance." Lois was impressed with her doctor's willingness to help. She said, "My doctor fought for me as an advocate with the insurance company."

Another discovery was the importance of the doctors who took extra time to strategize a game plan instead of rushing from one test or procedure to the next, providing little to no explanation for understanding on the part of the patient. Prayerful, thorough, sincere, and compassionate doctors and nurses made an impact for good on these women during frustrating and painful events.

A helpful strategy in a fertility clinic involves a staff liaison to guide patients and develop an overall plan to coordinate with the doctor. A team approach could go a long way towards helping patients holistically.

Physical

As illustrated in the opening story of this chapter, one of the more humiliating tests for couples involves the plastic specimen cup. There are many layers to this and often the wife struggles to approach her husband about having his sperm tested. This might conjure defensive emotions on both sides. Medical assistance and advice on this within the game plan would be helpful—having that testing introduced in a practical way as a standard test with no hint of blame, just investigating facts.

General patient care suggestions:

- *Please communicate accurate, up-to-date information to mitigate unnecessary stress. Make sure the labs you use are consistently testing and that no communication has been sent notifying your office that they no longer conduct certain tests.* The infertility ride is stressful enough without unnecessary humiliating speed bumps along the way.

- Provide support group resources or ask someone on your staff to coordinate occasional group meetings for patients to learn information and suggestions about outside emotional help.

- Offer quarterly workshops for your patients and bring someone in to conduct these. These could cover a variety of topics and be helpful for your patients.

- Conduct support training for medical staff. These occasional workshops can train staff for sensitivity to basic emotional and physical needs of their patients.

- Offer a team planning appointment with the patient, spouse, doctor, and a nurse.

- Provide resource cards for patients that include local workshops, counselors, etc.

Considering new, collaborative, caring outreach will serve your patients and their loved ones well.

Conclusion
A Note from the Author

My mom loves butterflies. She buys flowers and herbs to attract them—dill, rue, and butterfly weed have annual planting appointments in her patio pots and flowerbeds.

During the warm days of spring and hot summer days she watches closely for a variety of butterflies to lay their eggs and notes where they appear. Then begins the vigil for caterpillar growth (she holds fast to the belief that lizards and geckos are evil and they eat the eggs and tiny caterpillars if she isn't on duty for their protection).

She brings out swathes of netting to tie around larger plants with multiple caterpillars in order to protect the growing "children."

As soon as they are large enough, she brings each developing caterpillar on its twig inside to its condo—a clear glass bowl with net roof material held in place by a rubber band. Each caterpillar gets a daily meal of hand-gathered greens for nourishment. It is truly a butterfly bed and breakfast.

Eventually, the caterpillar stills on the twig or the side of the bowl and begins the chrysalis phase.

Many days later, the chrysalis darkens and this sends mom into the next phase of "baby" watch.

Miraculously, the ugly chrysalis eventually breaks open and a glorious butterfly emerges, wings rolled up and wet. This becomes the "hang time" stage. The butterfly must struggle to escape the small chrysalis, unfurl wings, and allow them time to dry. They might cling to the twig inside the bowl or hang upside down from their net ceiling. They allow their wings to hang open, with an occasional slow motion flutter to help dry. Usually a couple of hours go by and then, suddenly, the butterfly transitions to quick movement and restless activity.

Transformation complete, it is time to say goodbye.

The glass condo is carried outdoors, net gently removed, and my mom slowly puts her hand in to allow the butterfly to climb on her finger. He or she might stay for a few minutes or immediately fly off.

The new freedom and transformation is a wonder to behold.

Two transformations result from the caretaking of butterflies.

Sharing Wonder

I have watched my mom educate others on the stages and development. When the chrysalis condos line her counter and someone stops by for a visit, they usually leave with this unusual gift.

Giving others the opportunity to witness God's creativity is a gift she treasures. She passes them onto small children to cultivate a desire to learn about the world around us.

My mom also delivered these gifts to oncology nurses and patients when she herself went through cancer treatment.

What a life lesson in empathy and grace to all who see her acts.

Transformative Grief

The butterfly transformation process also reminds me of grief.

Picture yourself as a caterpillar, going along in daily living, gathering nourishment. Then something traumatic disrupts the routine and you surround yourself with isolation as a protective chrysalis.

When unexpected events, loss, and tragedies occur, part of the grieving process is to isolate and protect ourselves from further hurt and pain. If we don't pay close attention, we can build a thick, tough to break through "chrysalis" around ourselves.

Time apart from others can create healthy space as long as we pursue intentional healing. As the caterpillar is beautifully transformed within the chrysalis, so we can also experience positive transformation in the midst of our chrysalis post-life challenges.

The next time butterflies flutter by, be inspired and hopeful at the possibilities of transformation in the midst of life events.

If you have made it this far in the book, I assume you know someone in the midst of infertility and childlessness or possibly you are generally curious and want to help others. As you consider times of challenge and pain, spend a few minutes thinking about these questions:

Have you experienced chrysalis time in your life?
What did your transformation look like?

Thinking about your own life stories and how you felt or how someone compassionately reached out to you can illuminate ways for you to reach out to others.

The majority of this book is based on a research project and in-depth interviews that investigated experiences, encounters, and actions of real women in their infertility, loss, and involuntary childlessness.

Stories and details from these women helped develop real information to equip individuals and communities with an understanding of practical compassion.

The variety of pain experienced cannot be ranked. Those who were unable to get pregnant felt a lifetime question mark of *why* hanging over their heads. The women who endured miscarriage or infant loss owned an additional layer of devastation they worked through on their way to fruitful living.

The timeframe and manner in which each woman accepted her infertility differed. One conclusion drawn was the illumination of time:

No infertility experience and grief walk was the same. Everyone at the church and community table needed love and grace.

The interviewees were thrilled to be able to tell their stories and to have their voices heard—many for the very first time. They described individual versions of disappointment, confusion, and frustration with God. Time, wise counsel, prayer, study of Scripture, community support, and a realization of God's faithfulness played key roles in each woman's eventual acceptance of her situation and willingness to walk toward new fulfillment and opportunities.

I conducted the interviews, wrote and published the dissertation, and have now turned that information into this user-friendly book. I hope it provides more understanding and description of the complexities and ramifications of the infertility and involuntarily childless realities. I have also written and published a resource for women in the midst of the active infertility season, *Infertility & Involuntary Childlessness: Traveling the Terrain.*

Over varying lengths of time, these women have experienced positive and negative encounters and words through their cultures and communities. They hope that sharing their experiences will lead to better understanding and practical compassion.

Won't you help transform their journey by reaching out to offer practical compassion? Your understanding and care will resonate throughout their lives and accomplish much for God's kingdom work.

Endnotes

[1] U. S. Department of Health & Human Services, Office on Women's Health, "Infertility," accessed September 3, 2019, https://www.womenshealth.gov/a-z-topics/infertility#h.

[2] Pew Research Center Social & Demographic Trends, "Millennials in Adulthood," accessed September 8, 2015, http://www.pewsocialtrends.org/2014/03/07/millennials-in-adulthood/.

[3] Judith A. Stigger, *Coping with Infertility* (Minneapolis: Augsburg Publishing House, 1983), 30.

[4] Catherine, "Together Alone," *Still Standing Magazine*, accessed August 20, 2016, http://stillstandingmag.com/2016/08/together-alone/.

[5] American Society for Reproductive Medicine, "Defining Infertility," accessed September 26, 2015, http://www.reproductivefacts.org/uploadedFiles/ASRM_Content/Resources/Patient_Resources/Fact_Sheets_and_Info_Booklets/Defining%20infertility%20FINAL%20%202-19-14.pdf.

[6] Mayo Clinic, "Infertility," accessed October 7, 2015, http://www.mayoclinic.org/diseases-conditions/infertility/basics/definition/CON-20034770?p=1.

[7] Contrary to the researcher's view of the childless label, several sources including Jean W. Carter and Michael Carter, *Sweet Grapes: How to Stop Being Infertile and Start Living Again* (Indianapolis: Perspectives Press, 1998) and Sandra Glahn and William Cutrer, M.D., *The Infertility Companion: Hope and Help for Couples Facing Infertility* (Grand Rapids: Zondervan, 2004), present the transition

from childless to childfree, represented by the choice to move on from the "less" mentality.

[8] Glahn and Cutrer, *The Infertility Companion*, 247–8.

[9] Joseph H. Hellerman, *When the Church Was a Family: Recapturing Jesus' Vision for Authentic Christian Community* (Nashville: B & H Publishing Group, 2009), 119.

[10] Lydia Brownback, *Proverbs: A 12-Week Study* (Wheaton: Crossway, 2014), 87.

[11] Harvard Health Publications, "The Psychological Impact of Infertility and its Treatment," May 2009, accessed August 20, 2016, http://www.health.harvard.edu/newsletter_article/The-psychological-impact-of-infertility-and-its-treatment. The report explores the origin of infertility cases and determines that most cases have a physiological cause that creates heartache and a psychological burden of distress.

[12] Ibid.

[13] "American Society for Reproductive Medicine," accessed October 7, 2015, http://www.reproductivefacts.org/Psychological_FAQs/.

[14] Richard Winter, *When Life Goes Dark: Finding Hope in the Midst of Depression* (Downers Grove, IL: InterVarsity Press, 2012), 88.

[15] Harvard Health Publications, *The Psychological Impact of Infertility and its Treatment.*

[16] Glahn and Cutrer, *The Infertility Companion*, 73.

[17] Ibid., 73.

[18] Ibid., 74.

[19] Donna VanLiere, *Finding Grace: A True Story About Losing Your Way in Life…and Finding It Again* (New York: St. Martin's Press, 2009), 149.

[20] Justine Brooks Froelker, *Ever Upward: Overcoming the Lifelong Losses of Infertility to Own a Childfree Life* (New York: Morgan James Publishing, 2015), 42. Froelker's story in the book offers insight into her emotional and spiritual choices that contributed to a continued, hope-filled journey with Christ.

[21] Pamela Mahoney Tsigdinos, "Accepting Childlessness After Infertility," accessed August 20, 2016, https://www.seleni.org/advice-

support/article/accepting-childlessness-after-infertility. The author then describes the concept of *disenfranchised grief* as grief that is not acknowledged by society. She acknowledges her journey to actively mourning her losses and her recovery and peace finding.

[22] Kathe Wunnenberg, *Grieving the Child I Never Knew: A Devotional for Comfort in the Loss of Your Unborn or Newly Born Child* (Grand Rapids: Zondervan, 2015), 19.

[23] Melanie Notkin, *Otherhood: Modern Women Finding a New Kind of Happiness* (Berkeley, CA: Seal Press, 2014), xv. The author provides information from the U.S. Census publication Fertility of American Women: 2010. Of all American women of childbearing age, 47.1 percent do not have children of their own, married or not.

[24] American Society for Reproductive Medicine, "Fact Sheets and Info Booklets," 4, accessed October 7, 2015, http://www.reproductivefacts.org/uploadedFiles/ASRM_Content/Res ources/Patient_Resources/Fact_Sheets_and_Info_Booklets/agefertility .pdf. This report further details the decline in fertility (even premenopausal) in a woman's mid-forties and how this reality may affect any fertility treatments and procedures. Many young women mistakenly believe that they may benefit from the science of reproduction at any age.

[25] Travis M. Andrews, "It's Official: Millennials have Surpassed Baby Boomers to Become America's Largest Living Generation," accessed August 23, 2016, https://www.washingtonpost.com/news/morning-mix/wp/2016/04/26/its-official-millennials-have-surpassed-baby-boomers-to-become-americas-largest-living-generation/.

[26] Sandra Glahn and William Cutrer, M.D. *When Empty Arms Become a Heavy Burden: Encouragement for Couples Facing Infertility* (Grand Rapids: Kregel Publications, 2010), 130.

[27] M. Gay Hubbard, *More Than an Aspirin: A Christian Perspective on Pain and Suffering* (Grand Rapids: Discovery House Publishers, 2009), 144.

[28] René explained this concept of identity theft was a reference she learned in Bible Study Fellowship, an international, nondenominational Bible study.

[29] Margaret Mowczko, "Is Motherhood the Highest Calling for Women," *New Life*, March 9, 2011, accessed September 26, 2015, http://newlife.id.au/equality-and-gender-issues/is-motherhood-the-highest-calling-for-women/.

[30] John Eldredge and Stasi Eldredge, *Captivating: Unveiling the Mystery of a Woman's Soul* (Nashville: Thomas Nelson, Inc., 2010), 178–9.

[31] VanLiere, *Finding Grace*, 96–97.

[32] Glahn and Cutrer, *The Infertility Companion*, 77.

[33] Ibid., 247.

[34] Glahn and Cutrer, *When Empty Arms*, 131.

[35] Ibid.

[36] Laurie Lisle, *Without Child: Challenging the Stigma of Childlessness* (New York: Routledge, 1999), 182.

[37] Joan Jacobs Brumberg, *The Body Project: An Intimate History of American Girls* (New York: Random House, 1997).

[38] Mary Lemonwater, Lemonwater Blog, "The Hidden Emotions of Infertility," January 30, 2014, accessed September 16, 2015, https://lemonwaterblog.com/2014/01/30/the-hidden-emotions-of-infertility/.

[39] Hubbard, *More Than An Aspirin*, 232.

[40] Ibid., 232–3.

[41] There are supportive Christian websites and blogs that are helpful and comforting for those in the midst of infertility. Loving one another and making disciples enables believers in Jesus Christ to live out the Great Commission found in Matthew 28:19–20 and the Great Commandment in Matthew 22:37–40.

[42] Stacy Halstead, "Tripp Halstead Updates," August 24, 2014, accessed August 25, 2015, https://www.facebook.com/TrippHalsteadUpdates/photos/a.4739970

96011848.1073741827.371758639569028/696143483797207/?type
=3&theater.
[43] Susan Heavey, "Love, Marriage and Millennials—One More Look
at Fertility," accessed August 20, 2016,
http://healthjournalism.org/blog/2015/05/love-marriage-and-
millennials-one-more-look-at-fertility/.
[44] Reproductive Medical Associates of New Jersey, *Infertility in
America 2015,* 1, accessed August 20, 2016,
http://www.rmanj.com/2015/04/infertility-in-america-2015-survey-
report/. The report mentions the critical factor of age and infertility
and its related challenges and complications and the necessity of
Millennials to be aware of common misconceptions.
[45] Ibid., 2.
[46] Erika Janes, *Parents Magazine,* "What Millennials Think About
Infertility," accessed August 20, 2015,
http://www.parents.com/blogs/parents-perspective/2015/04/20/the-
parents-perspective/what-millennials-think-about-infertility/.
[47] Elinor Burkett, *The Baby Boon: How Family-Friendly America
Cheats the Childless* (New York: The Free Press, 2000), 180.
[48] Sumaira H. Malik and Neil S. Coulson, "Coming to Terms with
Permanent Involuntary Childlessness: A Phenomenological Analysis
of Bulletin Board Postings," *Europe's Journal Of Psychology* 9, no. 1
(February 2013): 84, accessed October 2, 2015, *Academic Search
Complete,* EBSCO*host.*
[49] Moss, Candida and Joel S. Baden. *Reconceiving Infertility: Biblical
Perspectives on Procreation and Childlessness* (Princeton, NJ: Princeton
University Press, 2015), 230-1.
[50] Moss and Baden, *Reconceiving Infertility,* 232.
[51] Hubbard, *More Than An Aspirin,* 23–24.
[52] Stigger, *Coping with Infertility,* 32.
[53] Hubbard, *More Than An Aspirin,* 133.
[54] Patricia S. Taylor, "One Question I Decided to Stop Asking and
Why You Should Too," *Seed Bed,* August 22, 2016, accessed August

22, 2016, http://www.seedbed.com/one-question-i-decided-to-stop-asking-and-why-you-should-too/.

[55] Melissa Ford, *Navigating the Land of IF: Understanding Infertility and Exploring Your Options* (Berkeley: Seal Press, 2009), 283.

[56] Mowczko, *Is Motherhood the Highest Calling for Women.*

[57] Glahn and Cutrer, *When Empty Arms*, 131.

[58] Ibid.

[59] Stigger, *Coping with Infertility*, 101.

[60] Barry Jones, "The Dinner Table as a Place of Connection, Brokenness, and Blessing," *DTS Magazine* 1, no. 1 (Fall 2015), accessed October 8, 2015, http://www.dts.edu/read/a-place-at-the-table-jones-barry/.

[61] Hubbard, *More Than An Aspirin*, 146.

[62] Rachel Giles, "Blessed, But Not with a Child," Health Section, *Church Times UK*, May 1, 2015, accessed August 20, 2016, https://www.churchtimes.co.uk/articles/2015/1-may/features/features/health-blessed-but-not-with-a-child.

[63] Hubbard, *More Than An Aspirin*, 34.

[64] Glahn and Cutrer, *The Infertility Companion*, 75.

[65] Moss and Baden, *Reconceiving Infertility*, 141.

[66] Beverly Hislop, *Shepherding Women in Pain: Real Women, Real Issues, and What You Need to Know to Truly Help* (Chicago: Moody Publishers, 2010), 88.

[67] Winter, *When Life Goes Dark*, 101.

[68] Ellen L. Walker, *Complete Without Kids: An Insider's Guide to Childfree Living by Choice or by Chance* (Austin: Greenleaf Book Group Press, 2011), 87.

[69] Terri Stovall, *Infertility: Where Grief Meets Grace*, Biblical Woman, February 2, 2012, accessed August 20, 2016, http://biblicalwoman.com/infertility-where-grief-meets-grace/.

[70] Hislop, *Shepherding Women in Pain*, 87–88.

[71] Marni Rosner, "Recovery from Traumatic Loss: A Study Of Women Living Without Children After Infertility" (DSW diss., University of Pennsylvania, 2012), 151, accessed August 20, 2016,

http://repository.upenn.edu/edissertations_sp2/20. Rosner's work focuses on effects of living without children after experiencing infertility and discovered great implications in subjects' relationships and identities.

[72] Stigger, *Coping with Infertility*, 90.

[73] Glahn and Cutrer, *The Infertility Companion*, 85.

[74] Hubbard, *More Than An Aspirin*, 260.

[75] Jill Bialosky and Helen Schulman, eds., *Wanting a Child: Twenty-Two Writers on Their Difficult but Mostly Successful Quests for Parenthood in a High-Tech Age* (New York: Farrar, Straus and Giroux, 1998), 4.

[76] Dennise Kraus, "Orthodox Church in America," October: Pregnancy and Infant Loss Awareness Month, vol. III (2010), accessed October 15, 2015, https://oca.org/parish-ministry/familylife/october-pregnancy-and-infant-loss-awareness-month.

[77] Pam W. Vredevelt, *Empty Arms* (Portland, OR: Multnomah Press, 1984), 50.

[78] Dawn Friedman, "Pregnancy Infant Loss," *Building Family Counseling*, accessed August 20, 2016, http://buildingfamilycounseling.com/2015/10/pregnancy-infant-loss/.

[79] Laura Seftel, *Grief Unseen: Healing Pregnancy Loss Through the Arts.* (London: Jessica Kingsley Publishers, 2006), 140–141, *eBook Collection (EBSCOhost)*, EBSCO*host* (accessed July 20, 2015).

[80] Deena Prichep, NPR, *Adopting a Buddhist Ritual to Mourn Miscarriage, Abortion*, August 15, 2015, accessed October 15, 2015, http://www.npr.org/2015/08/15/429761386/adopting-a-buddhist-ritual-to-mourn-miscarriage-abortion.

[81] Hislop, *Shepherding Women in Pain,* 88.

[82] Stigger, *Coping with Infertility*, 99.

[83] Brownback, *Proverbs: A 12-Week Study*, 87.

www.ingramcontent.com/pod-product-compliance
Lightning Source LLC
LaVergne TN
LVHW041252080426
835510LV00009B/707